PEARLS  WISDOM

PEARLS *of* WISDOM

Real Talk & No **BS** Insights to Transform
Your Love Life

MELANIE VERSTRAETE

Briton Publishing, LLC
810 Eastgate North Dr., Suite 200
Cincinnati, Ohio 45245
www.britonpublishing.com

ISBN: 978-1-956216-22-6

Briton Publishing books are distributed by Ingram Content Group and made available worldwide.

To my parents, George and Darlene—my greatest role models for life and love. I love you.

To my children—I love you endlessly; you are perfect exactly as you are, and it is my honor to be your mother.

To all who have touched my life—every one of you has been a sacred gift in my awakening (yes, even the exes).

To the past versions of me—thank you for your courage to walk this path and become the woman I am today.

To Rob and Brinka—your wisdom and support in bringing this first book to life will forever be appreciated.

And to God—for your love and direction, for without Your Love, nothing and no one would exist.

You don't have to hit rock bottom to make a change.

CONTENTS

Not Perfect, Just Obsessed

I am not perfect. I'm a human just like you. I am not your guru and I am not any better than you. I was you; I am you.

I have not had the most perfect, easy fairytale life; in fact, it's been quite the opposite. I am a person who struggled for as long as I can remember to feel loved, to feel like someone, anyone, preferably my mom and dad would be there for me. To feel like I mattered and belonged, like I was important to the people I felt were important, and for my love to be reciprocated, honored, cherished, and valued.

But instead, I felt unloved, discarded, and unimportant for the majority of my life. Unknowingly seeking to be loved and accepted by changing who I was to fit the version of me that my mom needed me to be, that my family needed me to be, that society needed me to be, that my multiple stepdads needed me to be, that boyfriends needed me to be, and that both of my ex-husbands needed me to be.

Do you know what that got me? Misery, exhaustion, self-loathing, attracting assholes who would treat me terribly, sacrificing myself to make others happy to the detriment of myself, people pleasing, zero boundaries, low self-worth, and a whole lot of thinking, *what is wrong with me?!*

And that made me wonder and seek to figure out who Melanie is, anyway?

That quest began over 7 years ago, of me determined, no, actually *obsessed* with fixing what I felt was broken in me, of figuring out who I am. I was working on myself like it was my *job*. It was during that time that I found the greatest gift, the Truth, and the treasures. I discovered the answers and became a master of my craft, transforming my life and relationships first and helping thousands of others, too.

So who am I?

I'm the person who helps you stop dating jerks and assholes (aka toxic relationships) and *finally* get into a relationship with someone amazing!

Be, Do, Have

Who are you *be*-ing? The name of this game of life is to *be*, to *do*, and then, to *have*. For a long time, we have been confused about this. We think we first do the thing (take action) and then we have the thing and then we will be happy or whatever fill in the blank for "happy" So many of us are obsessed with "the having," the possession of it all, the money, the power, the girl or guy, the relationship, the car, etc. But you cannot *have* what you are *not* within (who you are *be*-ing). This is Law. Not man's law, it's *Universal Law*, it's *God's Law*.

Ask yourself, *What do I really want?* Is it the true love of your life, your King or Queen? Maybe it's a better relationship with your family or better friends or a better relationship with your work colleagues or your clients? Whatever it is, *be* it. If you want more love in your life, *be* loving. If you want to be in a beautiful relationship, have a beautiful relationship with yourself. If you want more happiness in your life, *be* happy. If you want better friends, *be* a good friend yourself. You see, it all begins and ends with you. It's always a choice.

Now ask yourself, *Who do I have to be to have what I really want?* Operate with that mindset every day and watch how things change for the better. Watch how who you are *be*-ing creates the "having" effortlessly.

Who are you choosing to *be* today and every day?

Untamed and Unapologetic

In case you forgot: You are *wild... never* to be tamed.

You are real, you are raw, you are wild, you are unhinged, you are love, you are light, you are authentic, you are powerful, you are perfectly made in God's image, you are truth, you are beauty, you are pleasure, you are peace, you are freedom, you are joy, you are abundant, you are an EPIC human and don't you ever forget it! Be the weirdest, most unique, realest most magnificent you... the world has enough replicas. The Real you is who you came here to be. There is only one. You are rare. Start acting like it.

Now go shine that bright light!!!

Unconditionally Loved

You are love — pure, boundless, and infinite. From the moment you were created, you were woven from the very fabric of love itself, untouched and untainted. It's your essence, your core, the truest part of who you are. Today, let that love flow. Be gentle and kind with yourself, knowing you deserve the same care you so freely give others. Extend that love to humanity, to the animals that walk this earth, and to the earth itself, which nurtures us all. Give love without hesitation, without fear of it running out — because love is endless. And just as importantly, receive it. Open yourself to it fully.

Put down that guard you've built — those invisible walls meant to protect you from hurt. The only thing they're keeping out is the very love your soul craves. You don't need those walls anymore. It's safe to let love in.

And in case no one has reminded you today: I love you. Yes, you. Just as you are, in all your messy beauty. You're worthy of love, not because of what you do, but because of who you are. Now go out and share that truth with the world — because love, when given and received, is what heals us all.

Kick the Crap to the Curb

Why do we get into unhealthy, toxic relationships anyway? Why do we settle in our relationships? Why do we stay in relationships that make us feel less than?

One reason. You have an unhealthy, toxic relationship with yourself. I know because this used to be me, too.

- I used to people-please.
- I used to put other people's needs ahead of mine.
- I used to say yes when I really wanted to say no.
- I used to care more about what others thought of me than what I thought about myself.
- I used to shut my mouth when I really wanted to tell someone off for how they treated me.
- I used to talk shit to myself and be my own worst enemy.
- I used to lie there silent when all I wanted to do was scream.
- I used to have sex out of obligation when all I really wanted to do was to be left alone.
- I used to play the victim.

Do any of these sound like you?

Here's how to start changing this relationship with yourself so you can start to have the relationship of your dreams with others and kick those toxic relationships to the curb for good!

- Choose yourself first and always
- Speak up
- Say no when you want to say yes or vice versa
- Hold your boundaries
- If someone mistreats you, call them on it

Create a self-care, self-love practice, your "me time" that is non-negotiable. Examples are meditating, working out, massages, baths, time in nature, literally whatever makes you feel like you are caring for yourself. Do this every single day. Make it your non-negotiable. I spend a minimum of one hour a day doing this. Start small daily, try maybe 15 minutes a day. Once you make a plan or a decision to do it, it is important to choose an amount of time that you know you can and will commit to. And then you can build up from there once it becomes a habit.

No More Victim

You are the only problem you will ever have and *you* are the only solution.

Now hold on before you become unhinged.

I know you had some things that happened to you (it actually happened *for you*) meaning maybe you didn't have the greatest upbringing, or came from a "broken home," or your dad or mom wasn't in your life, or if they were they weren't the best role models, or maybe you had trauma in your past or have been in toxic relationships where you have been mistreated or even abused, or maybe you grew up poor, etc., etc.

Believe me, I get it and I get *you*.

If you've gone through some survival times in your past, trust me when I tell you I've been there too and had a train wreck of a past in more ways than you know. I get you because I've been you in many ways. And I could have stayed stuck in my story about how all the things that happened were not my fault.

Play the victim and say...

They were my mom's fault, my dad's fault, 'the economy's fault, society's fault, the president's fault, an ex-husband's fault, a bully's fault, and it all could be true, but here's the thing, only *you* can change it.

If you keep reliving in your mind all the "wrongs" that happened in your story you become addicted to that story.

Your story could be:

You came from a "broken home" therefore you are doomed to be broken.

You just have a bad picker and pick all the wrong people who treat you badly You think, *well, this is just my life, the cards I was dealt, I'm just not lucky like them.*

You have to stay married "for the kids" because *it's the right thing to do,* even though you know the marriage is unhealthy, because what would "they" think. The list could go on and on!

Do me, you, and the world a favor today. Change the story! Look in the mirror. Literally, look at yourself in the mirror. Look into those beautiful eyes, right into your soul, and ask yourself: are you living your life for *you* or everybody else?

What do you love? What lights you up? What turns you on? What speaks to your heart?

Make a new choice, a new decision, and create a new story by doing more of those things, and watch how the world around you responds in the most beautiful way!

Here's to creating a new story!

Shining in the Darkness

There used to be a time when I was worried about the relationship I had with my kids. You see, they were my everything when they were born. My first experience of loving another human at first sight.

I grew up not really feeling loved. I was told "I love you" a lot, but I never felt true. It always felt like strings attached. I'll love you if you do this or that, or if you are like this or that. It always felt fake, inauthentic.

But I buried it, because I was really good at that, suppressing feelings to stop the pain. Being numb was so much better than the alternative; giving your heart only to have it squashed, abandoned, or not reciprocated.

When I made the decision to leave my first toxic marriage to their father the *only* thing I thought about was them my children. I could stay because society told me, "It's the right thing to do." I certainly didn't want to be judged and then perpetuate the toxic patterns that had been going on in my family for generations and teach my daughter that being emotionally abused is just part of the gig with men and she should self-sacrifice for their benefit. And be the example for my boys of how to disrespect and disregard the feminine and create more toxic masculinity.

Or, I could leave. Set a new standard. A new reality. A new example. A better role model. One based on love, peace, freedom, joy, gratitude, faith, abundance, success, power, authenticity, kindness, purpose, generosity, and in service of something far greater than me. God.

That really pissed him off; to say the least, he stalked me, 4 personal protection orders later, and more drama than 100 lifetimes. He tried his hardest to get my kids to hate me. Didn't work.

Today, I have the most beautiful relationship with myself, my kids, my family, friends, clients, the earth, the animals, nature, humanity, and of course God.

I share this story with you in hopes that it inspires you to not stop, and never quit, even when it feels like life is kicking your ass and you feel like life sucks because it felt like that for me for most of my life. All things that happen are lessons. Lessons to teach you who you truly are.

You, my friend, are a beautiful, powerful, incredible, unique, rare, magical, epic human.

Shine that light and keep your beautiful heart open. I love you.

Your Relationships are Just a Selfie

I want to scream this from the rooftops!!!

Here's the real truth about relationships that most people won't tell you or maybe they don't even know themselves because it cuts deep: The quality of your relationships is *always* a direct reflection of the relationship you have with yourself.

LOVE is Always the Answer

For a long… long… long… time I did not love myself. I didn't know who I was, so how could I love myself?

I thought I was broken. I thought I was unworthy of love. I thought I was unlovable.

Parts of me were good enough and lovable and other parts were not, so they were deemed unlovable, unworthy, bad.

The lovable parts were that I was a good girl. I followed the rules, and I stayed in the box. I was never too much of anything. I played small and safe and never shined too brightly for fear of judgment or not being perceived as good. Not wanting to offend, putting others' needs always ahead of my own. I was the "good girl". The good wife, the good mom, the good daughter, the good employee, the good friend, etc., etc.

Turns out, trying to be everyone else's version of good, left me depleted from ever being good to the person who mattered the most… *me*.

All parts of me. The dark and the light, the healed and the wounded.

Not just the "good" girl, but the "bad" girl, too. Guess what? "Good and bad" are only perceptions.

Radical self-love for *all* parts of me was the answer. And it's the answer for you too.

From Meh to Magnificent

This changed everything for me.

To change your life for the better, you have to change how you think, how you feel, and what you believe.

This does not happen overnight. It requires consistent focus, practice, and attention. If you continue to think, believe, and feel as you have always been, nothing can change. You will continue to be what you have been.

To make any changes in our lives no matter if it's a better relationship with family and friends, a beautiful healthy romantic relationship, finding our purpose, living a life of more wealth and freedom, having inner peace, achieving success in our careers, truly anything we are desiring to experience in our lives first starts with our thinking.

We tend to think the same kind of thoughts over and over again out of habit and it's usually negative. I know mine definitely was. It's easy to think this way, it takes very little effort because look around you, it's everywhere... negativity. It's easy to go down that "rabbit hole." But *you* get to choose how and what you think is "good" or "bad." The choice is always yours. This takes consistency, practice, focus, and attention.

Here's how to start:

- Notice your thoughts without judgment, like a bystander.
- Notice how they feel in your body. What emotions do they bring out?
- Notice the beliefs you have about yourself, about the people around you, about your environment, about your life.
- Did you choose those thoughts, feelings, and beliefs? Or were they given to you by default due to your environment?

Simply just "noticing" is bringing awareness to it. Begin challenging your thoughts, feelings, and beliefs. If they are not serving the greatest good for you and those around you, change them into ones that do. These are the beginning keys to transformation.

They are the core principles the best of the best mentors I have worked with have taught me. And have completely transformed my life in the most ineffable ways.

And *you* can do it too!

The Boss Babe Lie

Boss babe culture is toxic and BS.

This might be pretty triggering, but like I always say our triggers are our teachers.

It needs to be said.

This BS needs to transform and alchemize. Before I get deeper into it, let me give you *my* definition of a boss babe because some could say, "Well aren't you a boss babe, Melanie?" Nope. I am so many things I cannot put myself in any one box. I do not fit in the box or any mold. I am ever-expanding. As are you.

Boss babe definition (my perspective): a woman who is successful in her career, she does all the things, maybe she stays late, and goes in early, very much into "taking massive action" in her life. She pushes. She is a do-er. She is a multitasking master. She can come off as cold or unfeeling, distant, guarded. She will never let you know how she is really feeling. If she isn't feeling well, she will pop a pill or suck it up and push past it. She looks at vulnerability as weak. She has a wall of protection up, her armor, and she wears it proudly. She can be many things such as an entrepreneur, CEO, or a high-level executive, runs her own business, is super independent, has a hard time asking for help or receiving help, her job title, or all these descriptives, it doesn't matter as much as her attitude does, which is…

"*I got this* and *I don't need you*" aka… a man.

She may even emasculate men saying that they are all assholes, liars, or cheaters, or they just want to "get in your pants." Sound familiar?

I used to be her. "I don't need you. I don't need a man. I can do all the things myself, haven't been able to lean on or trust you (any man in her life) anyway so I can do this all by myself."

And for the men reading this, maybe you've met this woman, dated her or married her. If you have, I'm sure you can relate.

Here's the challenge. This is false wounded energy, this is a fake mask to hide, shield, and protect your heart from the essence of the beautiful feminine being that you are. You weren't meant to *do it all* alone. Wanting an amazing man, a true partner, your soul's counterpart, does not make you weak. Wanting to be able to trust and feel safe, protected, and loved for all parts of you does not diminish your power as a woman. It does not dim your light. It actually allows your femininity, the essence of being a woman... to bloom, to blossom like a beautiful rose even more.

If you can't find, attract, or keep a "good" man maybe it's because *you are the man.*

This is repelling the very thing you yearn for, the very thing your heart longs to trust and open to and feel the love of this man.

We are not meant to do it all by ourselves, ladies. Can we? Absolutely. If we had to, but do you really want to?

I say nope. It's exhausting. Your power is not in all the action and doing, although we need that too at times, but to really embody what it means to be a feminine being, means to *be* in your body.

Feel the power of your sensuality (this doesn't make you a slut or any of that other toxic narrative BS), your creativity, your connection to the women around you in sisterhood, and your natural creativity. For God's sake, we create life in our wombs! Allow yourself to feel your flowy nature, your grief, your rage, your abundance, your compassion, your ability to trust and surrender, your fire, your wildness, your primal nature, all of your emotions. We have turned off too much of ourselves. Allow yourself to immerse into the naturalness of your menstrual cycle, your open and beautiful heart, your vulnerability, your authenticity, your nurturing, your connection to Mother Earth, your connection to God, and your creative expression through whatever lights you up. Allow yourself more opportunities to dance, and play. And have fun. I could go on and on.

BE-ing in your being... the true essence of your femininity... *that's your power, babe!*

Break the Molds: Be True, Be You

On many occasions in my life, I have been told, "I swear too much" I find this interesting and comical, and here is the teaching moment I want you to get in your own life if you are open to it:

First, are we five years old?! I thought we were adults.

Why would I change anything I do to fit into someone else's version of what feels good or right to them? Why would I morph myself into someone else's version of what they deem acceptable? Why would I change to a different version to make you more comfortable? That's the mere definition of fake or inauthentic. No thanks.

Where does it end?

Do you see that if you start to change who you are because someone else has a problem with who you are, the changing of you to fit their narrative will never end?

And then do you see if you start trying to please everyone else around you to make them happy/comfortable/less offended (fill in the blank) that then who do you become in all of this? Where is the *real* you in all of this, if all you are is a mixture of what everyone else wants you to be?

Do you see where this is going? No place you want to be, I promise you. This is the road to misery.

I lead; I do not follow the masses.

I swear because I want to, it's part of who I am, the *real* me, I enjoy it, it feels good, it is me being authentic to who I am. I say it how it is; many say that I say things that they only wish they could say. I tell them, you can do the same. What is stopping you? I don't swear to shock or to have a certain effect on you, I do it for me, it is part of me, my essence, and who I choose to be, not who I have been told to be. I speak my Truth and I always speak it with love, never to hurt or diminish, always to empower and to help you see the *real you*.

I am an activator, an inspirer, a disruptor and I am here to shake you awake to your own power, your own truth, your own divinity, the *real you* that is hidden underneath all the lies that we have been conditioned and brainwashed to believe about our powerlessness about fitting into a box or a mold that makes you controllable.

If you are triggered by anyone, understand that the trigger is your teacher, and you have two options:

1. You can leave, no one is forcing you to be wherever you are that you got triggered.

2. You can be with the trigger, feel it inside of your body, the sensation, and ask yourself, why am I triggered? What about this situation has me angry or upset?

And then wait for the answers from your own inner wisdom, your gut, your intuition, whatever you want to call it... listen for the answers. There is always something there, a gift, a lesson from within that we have not learned about ourselves yet. Let it reveal itself to you.

Life is a Wild Ride, Strap In

When did we stop having fun?

We are so serious, gloom, doom, the sky is falling Chicken Little crap. Our life is meant to be *lived,* not to hustle and grind until we die. I have a secret, *shhhh,* no one gets out of this alive.

I'm not saying life is not full of challenges, God knows I have had my share of plenty of those! But these challenges are not meant for you to take life so seriously, to get stuck in the story, they are there to open you, to allow you to surrender to this beautiful dance called life. Full of everything and it is not all love and light. And I think that is part of the problem because we think it should be. That's BS. It's full of light and dark, good and bad, love and grief, laughter and sadness, life and death, literally everything. And we signed up for this. You did, whether you realize it or not, your soul did. You wanted to experience the juicy realness of *all* things, all experiences, not just the rainbows and unicorns. Although we think that is the answer that is why many of us stop having joy and fun in our lives. Then where would be the contrast to appreciate the "good" if we couldn't compare it to the "bad".

You can still appreciate the richness of life when you are crying and grieving, in fact, I encourage you to. It's not a punishment and I think that's where a lot of us get stuck. We don't want to feel the tough feelings and emotions, it hurts too much so we chase after the higher ones, there is nothing wrong with either, but they all exist, the polarity of all that is. And we are told to stay away from those feelings because it "means something bad."

Do you know what it means? Truly, it means you are a human, that's it and you are here in earth school trying to do the best you can like everyone else. When we reject certain parts of our experience, we inhibit our ability to feel *all* of life. Here's a real-life example we can all relate to: a person breaks up with a partner or is broken up with, declares, "I will never love again" or some variation of that. So they armor up their heart, guard it against ever feeling that depth of grief again, and in doing so they have also guarded their heart against fully living and experiencing the real, raw, juicy depths of Be-ing that their soul came here to experience and the one thing they wanted more than anything else was to be loved and guess what, that armor, yea it keeps out the pain, *and* (more importantly) it keeps out the love.

My point to all of this, and this is a reminder that I often give myself, is to enjoy this life, have some fun, don't be so serious, and take a childlike attitude with the miracle of this gift of life you have been given.

Enjoy life, especially during the challenging times. Don't take yourself so seriously. Count your blessings, and appreciate the good times. Grieve your losses, look at the sunset and the stars, smell the fresh air, and spend time with the people you love. Eat the ice cream, skinny dip in the lake, take the day off, get in nature, love with all your heart, speak your truth, and be kind to your fellow humans and all creatures. Be kind to yourself, don't work too much, go on vacation, take a nap, laugh, and cry. Know that you, this life, and your experience is a sacred gift.

Not Everyone is a Self-Absorbed Asshole

Let's talk about narcissism for a moment. First, I just have to say that this is one of the most overused words in our culture right now and I wanted to offer a different perspective.

It seems like everyone is being labeled as a narcissist. And that in and of itself is so unhealthy. I'm not doubting people can have narcissistic behaviors or patterns, but it is not a "disease" in the way so many people like to talk about it or blame people for it. Not everyone is a narcissist. Okay?

I'm not here to defend or blame, just provide a different perspective. Because we all love to point our fingers and blame as a society, it is easier to put people into little boxes that label them and their behavior or actions as "good or bad." It makes us feel safe. It's not quite that simple though.

The dictionary defines narcissism as, "Personality qualities include thinking very highly of oneself, needing admiration, believing others are inferior, and lacking empathy for others."

Contrary to what many people think, those who have been in relationships with narcissists (my first husband definitely could have been labeled as a narcissist), or who themselves have narcissistic patterns or narcissistic behaviors when seen in adults can actually be a survival mechanism.

You might be saying, "WTF?! My ex was a total piece of crap narcissist and treated me terribly and I have gone to therapy for years because of him or her. They are the very reason I won't get into another relationship, etc." I can hear you now.

And these things could be true. But did you know that people who grow up to be narcissistic adults were once children who were abused, neglected, heavily criticized, or on the completely other side of that spectrum, they were overvalued, as in the parent/s treated their child as better than or superior to others. So, let's also examine ourselves as parents.

It is a pattern, a way of being, conditioned behavior during childhood years, as are many of our ways of being. I am not saying we should tolerate or accept this behavior towards ourselves or others. What I am saying is to have more compassion, open-mindedness, kindness, and more awareness. When did we get so mean towards each other anyway?

We are really all in this world together (is that a song?) in case you forgot, a gentle reminder. It is not you against me, me against them, him, or whatever to whomever. If we want to start living in harmony, more cohesiveness, more in alignment with our true nature, it starts with us, inside, you first, to start examining these so-called beliefs about everything, not just this subject. Question everything. Question this book. If it lands great, if it doesn't that's okay too, maybe try it on later.

Can we have some empathy and compassion with each other and ask if they are just unconsciously living out their childhood in adulthood in the only way they know how? And also taking your own responsibility in that relationship too. None of us are 100% innocent.

We all have toxic, unhealthy traits, it's part of being human until we become aware that they exist and then it is our responsibility to take radical self-accountability to heal those parts.

Narcissism is not an incurable disease, so let's stop talking about it like it is, it's also not an excuse to be an asshole. It is a learned conditioned behavior, sometimes a survival mechanism learned in childhood, that can be unlearned and a new way of being can be learned.

Let us all be more open to looking at things in a new light.

The Ultimate Elixir for Life's BS

Many people talk about gratitude, right? The importance of it is the "attitude of gratitude," but very few talk about why or how.

You may think:

- How can I be grateful when my world feels like it is falling apart?
- How can I be grateful when I hate my job or my boss?
- How can I be grateful when I am sick?
- How can I be grateful when I am lonely and just want my true love?
- How can I be grateful when my bank account is low and I'm struggling to pay the bills?
- How can I be grateful when all I seem to attract are toxic, unhealthy relationships?

First, because it feels good! When have you ever felt anything other than good when you felt gratitude for something?

Second, because everything in your life truly is a gift, seriously, nothing is happening to hurt or punish you, you are not broken, everything is literally for your greatest good and for the good of all. Even that terrible, difficult divorce or breakup, even that job loss, even the boss that pisses you off. I bet if you looked back in your past to some of the things that felt painful and terrible at the time, where you may have thought WTF, on the other side of that, was a lesson, a gift, a level up, some "thing" that needed to happen, even though it probably hurt like hell, to get you to see another side of your*self*, your truest most authentic expression of *you*.

You see, life is always conspiring for your greatest good. It reveals to you the parts of yourself that you have not seen.

I'll share a quick story about my experience with gratitude. When I was married to my second husband and was contemplating divorce,

I had that realization "What is wrong with me that I keep attracting these kinds of toxic men?" I felt deeply broken. And in that moment did I feel gratitude for the pain and suffering I was going through? No. I wasn't who I am now in my journey of healing and unbecoming. But looking back, that was the catalyst, that was the come to Jesus moment. It was the break within my psyche, the surrender that had to happen within me to start my journey of waking up. I am in deep gratitude for all of it because it helped me to become who I am today.

This is why I share my stories and experiences and everything I have learned, in hopes that you can learn the easy way.

Can you start opening your mind to feel more gratitude in every situation? Where I find we usually keep ourselves stuck in the loop of suffering or misery is when we focus too much on looking at our past and living in the "shoulda, woulda, coulda" space and/or living too much into the future thinking I have no idea how to get to "that or there" so I'm going to stress over the fear that it may never happen or maybe even give up entirely, and that's what you unconsciously create.

If you are a parent, think of it this way. Do you ever feel unappreciated by your children? Feels terrible right?

Have you ever felt unappreciated by your love interest, your family, your boss, your friends, your community, society, etc?

I think we have *all* felt deeply unappreciated by someone, probably many times over our lifetime. And how does it feel? Like crap, right? You may even think, "Forget this, I'm not doing anything else for this person."

So, let's pan out a bigger, larger, universe-level picture here. Here we all are given this beautiful gift called Life and we bitch and complain that it's not good enough. How does it feel when you feel deeply unappreciated? Not good, right?

Why should you feel grateful for this gift of Life? The vibration, frequency, and feeling of gratitude are some of the most powerful forces, in addition to love in the universe. It attracts more things to be grateful for.

So the next time you want to bitch, complain, and wallow in self-pity, ruminating in all the ways your life sucks, take a minute and reflect on what is actually true. I invite you to take this even a step further and do something I have my clients do.

Write down on a sheet of paper all the things you desire, but do not have yet.

Then on a separate sheet of paper write down all the things you do have or have had. Include everything, leave nothing out, especially things that are not actually "things" such as being healthy and having people in your life who love you, etc. Then compare the two.

I would bet the second list is *far* larger than the first. Gratitude. This always helps to keep things in perspective of the bigger picture. Try this and watch how your life starts to change for the better.

Not All Heroes Wear Capes

Can we all just take a moment to celebrate the ones doing the work to heal the negative patterns, belief systems, lies, toxicity, the unhealthy ways of being, those who are breaking the chain of all that pain that has run in their ancestral lineage?

That work is not easy, it is not for the faint of heart. For those of you that this speaks to, I want you to remember this:

- You are doing the work no one else in your lineage could do!
- You are the warriors!
- You are the courageous ones!
- You are badasses!
- You are so strong!
- You are shifting the collective consciousness!
- And don't you ever forget it!

This work may not always be seen visibly by all as an accomplishment or a "result" of a thing such as a relationship, a house, a luxury car, or a certain career. *But* this work is the work that changes the world! It radically shifts who we are within, our innermost selves, which causes changes to the "results" of our outside world for all!

I see *you*

I hear *you*

I feel *you*

I am *you*

I love *you*

The Hamster Wheel of Lies

Many of the things we learned growing up are complete BS and can keep us stuck on a hamster wheel of repeating the same mistakes over and over again.

Like for example, in relationships, why do we keep attracting the same kind of guy or girl? Why do we attract people who are emotionally unavailable? Why do we attract people who never have enough time for us? Why do we attract people who treat us like crap? Obviously, this can show up in any area of our lives, not just relationships. And in my experience and the experience of my clients, where this shows up in one aspect of our lives it can show up in many. Like in my life in the past, I attracted guys who made me feel unworthy. Why? Because down deep, deep, deep within me, that's what I believed to be true. I felt unworthy, not good enough.

Did I know that? Nope. Not in a conscious, practical mind way. This was not logical. This was deep conditioning, programming if you will that ran like an autopilot that I had absolutely no control over, yet it made *all* of my decisions, all of my choices. That sinister little belief that ran undetected was one of the main reasons my adult life was so painful. It was the epiphany of a painful yet second divorce that I had an awakening, the pain that accumulated over all those years was suddenly absolutely unbearable. It literally felt like God stepped in and said, change or die. It felt that dark, and also that light. I had to take a true, difficult look at who I had become and it was painful. Smacked awake.

Many beliefs, thoughts, and lies I completely bought into from my parents, stepdads, family, society, friends, colleagues, culture, television, movies, and even my ancestors, etc. This was all part of my autopilot. It controlled what kind of relationships I got into (most were super toxic and the ones that were good, well I sabotaged them out of fear that the person would suddenly realize I wasn't good enough and then dump me), it controlled how much money I made, it controlled what careers I chose, what I felt about myself which was not good, what I thought about others, the quality of my friendships. Literally everything. I had to unlearn *so much*. But when I did, *wow* my life started to completely shift for the better! My life became absolutely unrecognizable compared to how I was living and feeling my entire life. I felt free for the first time in my life! Like a bird who was just set free from its cage. And that's one of the many reasons I am so passionate about this work and this book. Because if I can go from a hot mess to having it all, so can you.

Your Inner Child May Be Sabotaging Your Love Life

Recently, I got into a discussion about what's killing marriages/relationships these days.

Now there are *a lot* of answers that can come from this question. Many believe it's social media, too many choices, single friends, lack of appreciation, unrealistic expectations, lack of commitment, unfaithfulness, in-laws, no trust, lack of God, the internet, extreme feminism, not being able to accept each other's flaws, men only want sex, women marry for money, and the list goes on.

The challenge here is we can play the blame game all we want, but none of these "reasons" that people give get to the root cause of all suffering in general and especially in romantic relationships and that is at its most simplistic answer: unhealed childhood wounds.

People are unconsciously, not actually choosing with their reasoning mind, they are choosing through their "autopilot" romantic partners who are similar to their childhood caretakers and who they believe can heal what they never received from their parental childhood caretakers.

The challenge is people will look to that person as their "savior" or solution, "the one who will make all my pain go away." When the partner does not meet those needs, not because they don't want to or they don't care, but because they can't be the father or mother you need, resentment occurs and eventually the relationship gets toxic.

The answer is to take radical responsibility for yourself and the needs that were never met and the healing needed and if that means a book, a mentor, a therapist, or whatever else feels good and right for you in your journey then you need to do it. Because no one can do this for you. Only you can make the decision to actually say yes to yourself and start.

Don't Fill the Void with a Decoy

Why do we settle in relationships?

Let me define how I see settling: choosing a partner that you know is not right for you, you know this to be true and feel deep down, even if you lie to yourself, nope they're not it, *buuuuut* you get in a relationship with them anyway.

Here's the danger in that. You are telling God, and the Universe, that you don't believe in what you say you desire in a partner, you don't believe that person exists, so you better just settle for this guy/girl. Hearing words like this in your head: "Don't be greedy, your standards are too high, you need to lower your standards, who do you think you are?" Does any of this sound familiar?

When doing that, this partner you settled for takes up the "space" energetically of the partner you really want, a partner who is right for you, basically not allowing the energy for the partner you really desire to come into your world. How's that for getting in your own way?!

This can perpetually keep you stuck in a cycle of unhealthy, unfulfilling relationships. The solution would be to be brave enough to ask and demand what you want in a partner and say no to anyone else who is not him or her.

Be courageous enough to stop unconsciously dating just to have something to do, to stop trying to fill the space of loneliness with any human that will pay attention to you.

Be courageous enough to hold the "void" of not having a partner.

Be courageous enough to be alone for a while if that's what it takes.

Be courageous enough to do the work to heal the past versions of you that have settled for being second choice, for choosing emotionally unavailable partners, for choosing those who don't choose you back.

Remember the more you say *no* to what is not for you, the faster the *yes's* and what is right for you can come into your life.

Dethrone the Jokers

You are meant to have a love that is pure. A providership rooted in deep surrender and truth. Yours and theirs. A relationship that makes your whole body tingle, while it brings peace to your soul. It should be a partnership that challenges you, expands you, excites you, and calls you into your higher self. Yet you have found yourself swimming in a dating pool of pee.

What does this look or feel like?

It looks like they constantly want and need more of you, from you, your energy, time, and resources, but it's not an equal energy exchange.

You don't receive the same level of devotion, commitment, connection, dedication, vision, and ambition from them. They show up with half-ass energy, half-ass intimacy, excuses, and a glass-half-empty mindset at all times.

It feels stagnant and heavy, and this cycle keeps replaying itself, like a record that has been scratched, and now it's stuck in inertia.

You find yourself in dynamics that have you mothering everyone — your partner/spouse, your children, your friends, your team, your clients. Is it any wonder that you feel weighed down?

As a result, your innate, sacred, and sensual magnetism is turned off. You've known for a while that something needs to shift and you know it starts with you. It doesn't start with your partner, your family, your children, your clients, or your team. *You* are the commonality.

If you're here reading this book, it's no coincidence. You're ready to rekindle your passion, ignite your fire, and activate momentum in your life. And I am here to guide you and ignite you on this homecoming to your soul. It is time gorgeous soul, to call in your King, so you can be the Queen, you know yourself to be.

.

The queen commands a room with her presence and her energy.

Without dimming her power, without suppressing her voice.

Without playing any games whatsoever.

It is time, to lead with your sensuality, your wild feminine, your softness, which becomes your strength, your magnum opus.

Changes in our lives don't happen by doing the same thing over and over again, this would be the definition of insanity, or by hoping and wishing. Changes happen when we *do* something different when we enter the unknown even and *especially* when it's scary. That's where the growth is!

Get Out of Your Own Damn Way

Two points of pain and challenges I see in our society and culture:

1. Lack of a connection with God (or whatever you want to call the Creator of everything)

2. Lack of taking responsibility for one's life and choices

I'm not here to preach religion to you. In fact, I think the way we were raised (conditioned, brainwashed) around religion is part of the reason we are disconnected from God. Religion teaches fear, hell, and a punishing God. For clarity, I am not talking about the original teachings of Yeshua aka Jesus.

To me, God is the pure essence of all of Life, The One, The Creator of all things, omnipotent and omnipresent, pure unconditional Love. There is no fear, lack, hate, worry, doubt, resentment, competition, poverty, limitations, or failures, in God.

Remember what is written on our money? *In God we Trust.* I wonder how life would be different if everyone remembered that? Do you trust that everything in your life is for your greater good? Or, do you believe everything and everyone is conspiring against you?

The greatest version of you is actually God working to and through you. Some call that your Higher Self. It is your True Self.

It is you *now*. It always has been, and it's available to you whenever you claim, accept it, and deny anything that is unlike itself.

We love to blame anything and everything about why our lives suck, why we can't find any good men or any good women, why we are not successful, why we are not rich, why we are sick, why we are not fit, the list goes on and on.

The reason you are not this way or that way is that you simply choose not to take responsibility for your life and your choices. It was that very thing that changed everything for me.

I will always remember these words that I said to myself after the realization of yet another divorce. Divorce number 2:

"What is wrong with you that you keep attracting and choosing toxic men?" I was the common denominator. *Me*. And at the time I felt broken, I know this is not true, however taking radical responsibility for myself and my actions and who I was being in the world was the catalyst for change that I needed to become the incredible woman I am today, able to lead and guide others back to their own power, their own Truth and divine nature.

Don't you think it's time you started taking responsibility for your own life? Yes, I know you can blame all kinds of things, and many are true and really part of your life, I get it, my past was loaded with trauma, pain, struggles, and just pure survival. But I can tell you, that is not why we are here. We are here to *thrive*. To live a life full of love, joy, fun, peace, growth, creativity, authenticity, health, and wealth — Heaven on Earth.

That is our True Nature. "The Father that dwelleth in me He doeth the works."

It starts with you though. What part of your life can you stop pointing your finger at , staying addicted to your old story, and start to take ownership back of your life? You have given away your power. Time to take it back. And your true power is getting the hell out of your own way and allowing God to work through you.

In God we Trust. I love you and I believe in you. You got this!

Where Have All the Real Men Gone?

Someone recently asked me: "Why do men find strong women intimidating?"

This was my answer:

Define "strong women"? Collectively many women had been conditioned to have to be strong to merely survive.

And then if you add to it any lack of trust in men from childhood or past negative relationships and now you have women being hyper-independent (I got this I don't need a man attitude) emasculating men and then wondering where all the good men are.

They have become "the man" therefore no real masculine man, the very kind of man she really desires wants her, in fact, he is repelled by her because she is "the man". The answers that I have found within myself, and for my clients, are for more women to understand they may be in "survival" defensive mode energy. They need to tap into their own innate powerful, beautiful feminine energies where she is naturally strong.

Also, I'll add men need to stop being so passive, and "the nice guy" afraid of his own strength and masculinity because the unhealthy toxic feminists have told him that his masculinity is bad, so he waffles and wavers from who he is and what he wants… out of fear of being too aggressive, so then he becomes too passive. A shell of the man he once was. Then we wonder where all the good men are. A feminine woman is repelled by a man like that. The polarity between the two energies must exist.

And you also have the "fuckboy", addicted to meaningless sex, quantity or quality, porn, vapes, partying, etc. draining his life force energy.

This division has been put here on purpose, time to pay attention, start thinking for yourself, and wake up. It's all part of the manipulation and breaking up of the family. Probably a topic for another conversation.

The polarity and alignment between the masculine and feminine energies is where the chemistry and the sparks live. If you are a woman lean into what makes you feel naturally feminine. If you are a man lean into what makes you feel naturally masculine…no matter what "they" say.

I See God in You, Even When You Don't

I don't play in the shallows. I can't stand small talk. I don't care what your favorite color is. I want to know your heart, your bare-naked soul, your humanity, and who you really are, raw and real.

Know that if you are in my life, or reading my book it's not by chance or a coincidence. Our souls have chosen this. And I will take you into the deepest parts of yourself, as a friend, a lover, a husband, and a client, it makes no difference what relationship we have. If I accept you into my world, then you are a full *yes* to me.

I cannot unsee who you really are and cannot keep quiet about that to you. I must share what I see within you.

I see deeper into the parts of you than most. I see past the masks, the doubts, the pain, the limitations, the lies you believe about yourself. I see God within you, even when you don't.

I will call you out and call you forward.

I will not let you stay stuck in your story and play the victim. You are not your past. And at the same time, I will hold you with the deepest reverence and compassion for your pain.

I will probably make you feel uncomfortable. To that, I say good because your greatest good lives within the uncomfortable.

I will help you to remove the invisible chains, the boxes, and the walls you have created around yourself unknowingly to keep you safe.

And in all of that, I am your best friend, your biggest cheerleader, and your greatest ally.

This is my magic.

The Rebel's Guide to Self-Respect

Do no harm *and...* take no shit!

Your purpose wasn't and isn't to serve as a whipping post for the pain of others. Many people, women especially feel we have to love and nurture no matter what, and give of ourselves to depletion, to emptiness, to exhaustion for our kids, for our family, for our careers. That's not who you are here to be.

This does not make you a "bad person," although the people who are benefiting from that will definitely make you feel like you are the bad person, the selfish jerk, that you only care about yourself. They manipulate you and play into your guilt of wanting to be liked and accepted.

I'm not saying we are here to be selfish assholes, although sometimes being an asshole could be appropriate, but we are also not here to be martyrs, victims, the scapegoats, or the reason why "you did this to me or made me do this" kind of crap. This allows people to suck the life out of us for their own benefit. Open your eyes to the conditioning you have been operating under. It's not the real you.

I used to take *a lot* of crap from people, well most of it anyway. From my mom, mothers-in-law, husbands, step-kids, people who acted like my friends but were more like frenemies, bosses, and pervy guys who talked to me like I was an object put here for their benefit. Don't get me wrong, I would occasionally speak up, but only to be "put back into my place." Who do you think you are, Melanie?! This left me feeling empty, exhausted, sad, alone, fearful, and unworthy, a feeling of continuous "what's wrong with me?"

Have you been there?

I'm curious, do you give of yourself unconditionally because you feel it's your duty as a mom or a dad or a wife or a husband, an employee or employer, etc.? This can be more prominent in women sometimes.

Do you allow others to take advantage of your good nature and mistake your kindness for weakness and yet you don't speak up?

Do you allow the fear of criticism, judgment, or hurting people's feelings rule your life, so you shut your mouth and don't speak up? Instead, you stay silent, taking it, thinking it doesn't matter anyway?

Do you follow and believe the people in charge or of some sort of presumed "authority figure" simply because they present themselves as "leaders," or do you question everything, do your own research to learn and think for yourself?

One of the many truths I have learned in my own unbecoming and healing is that God, the Creator, Infinite Intelligence... whatever you choose to call The One who created everything that is and everything that ever will be... I call this God... yea, God did not put you here to be people's punching bag.

You are not a whipping post.

You are just as important as "they" are.

You are a multi-faceted, multi-talented being who came here to shine your light as the biggest, brightest, bad-assed-est (my made-up word!) most authentic expression of you and your unique gifts. Your medicine. Your magic. Your fullest expression.

Your Worth isn't Measured in Dollars

Okay, this needs to be said. No one talks about this and it is important.

Coaches, mentors, and anyone else selling this idea stop telling people that they can make 6, 7, 8, and 9-figure incomes if they take your program.

There. I said it.

Now let me dig into this a little bit more before you lose it, although I am sure many of you already have. Here is the problem I have with this BS, and I too just so you know have bought into this web of lies, so I know first-hand this experience. Who I am in this world is the person who goes through love and relationship challenges and comes out on the other side and then teaches you how to do the same.

So, this is me being me here for y'all, as always.

This kind of marketing can cause more harm and trauma than good in some instances.

I do believe we are all unique, powerful, beautiful, special people, created by God. I also believe we have unlimited potential that we cannot even fathom tapping into in this lifetime.

I know that because we are all so unique (there is truly only one of you!) and our souls have all chosen to have unique lives and unique experiences. Making millions of dollars is not necessarily the Truth for every person!

One of the many things that I have learned over the years within my own healing and unbecoming, is that what one person chooses to experience does not mean it is good or right for everyone. Also known as, *to each his own.*

I had some *deep* wounds around money and it *did not matter* how many courses I took, how much money I spent (and I spent *a lot*) to learn how to become this 6, 7, 8, 9-figure earner, *none of it worked.* None of it! And I'm not afraid to share this with you, in fact, I know it is actually my duty, my responsibility to share this with you because many are struggling and getting hurt from this, many are getting re-traumatized, many are actually perpetuating not having money while creating more debt and scarcity, many are thinking they must just not be worthy or good enough, so they must be screwed up or broken, because they are comparing themselves to everyone else that is *supposedly* millionaires (many of this is fake too, many who are teaching you how to become a millionaire are not millionaires themselves, saying that they are so that you'll buy their program). Please understand this is not a knock to the coaching industry, there are plenty of gifted excellent coaches/mentors out there.

Know this: There is nothing wrong with you if you are not rich in terms of money *and* there is nothing wrong with you if you are.

Sometimes who you chose to be in this lifetime doesn't align with being rich, sometimes your relationships are what matter to you most, sometimes your health and body are what matter to you most, and sometimes being a parent is what matters to you most, sometimes your career is what matters to you most, sometimes being a monk is what matters to you most, sometimes being the warrior in your family's lineage and healing the past ancestors and therefore the future too from the toxicity that has run in your family for generations is what matters to you most… you are each uniquely different here to express yourself fully as *who you truly are,* in your most authentic expression.

You and I are not the same, nor should we be. How boring life would be if we were all the same, yet that is the box we are sold isn't it? To try to be like everyone else to "fit in" and be liked.

And also, I will add, that many people have deep wounds around money, deep trauma that runs through their ancestral lineage that can take *years* to heal. Not one course, one coach, one Kambo ceremony, one Ayahuasca ceremony, one retreat, one therapist, one book, one podcast… this work is deep and takes devotion and persistence and also humility, surrender, courage and time actually doing the work. I know this intimately and I have done *a lot* of work unpacking this, as this too runs deep in my ancestral lineage, and because of this, that is why I am writing this to you.

You are not here to fit into any box. Your genius cannot be contained. Allow this book to be your permission slip to be the most authentic expression of you, and that may involve being rich where you make all the money and that may involve something completely different entirely.

Be brave enough to be *you*, no matter what. The world needs your unique expression.

"I Don't Need A Man" Is Killing Your Love Life

Why do strong, independent women have a hard time finding a real man?

This seems to be so common today and really has men and women at odds with each other.

Hating on each other, battling, competing. It's not natural and it's not the way it's supposed to be in healthy relationships.

But that doesn't change the fact that it is something very real that we are seeing and struggling with in today's modern love, dating, and relationship world.

The challenge is that many women today who are very strong and independent have been conditioned, wired, (whatever word works for you) to be this way out of necessity for survival, imprinted biologically on their nervous system when they were children.

This can be for a multitude of reasons. Some because they simply were abandoned by their father at an early age, or their father did not have much to do with them, or he worked all the time and placed very little value on her and their relationship. Basically, the relationship with her male caretaker, usually her father, was incomplete, missing altogether, or inadequate.

I am not pointing fingers or trying to place any blame here. All of our parents did the best they could with what they knew and who they were at the time. My intention is to educate to create understanding.

She would have probably been forced to grow up early, sometimes as a child, she may have even taken on the caretaker role herself; child parenting the parent or having to parent herself.

She may not have even had much of a joyful childhood and she may even have missing parts and pieces in her memory of her childhood, usually an indication of past trauma/pain/lack of safety.

According to Maslow, our hierarchy of needs are physiological, safety, belonging and love, social needs or esteem, self-actualization, and transcendence. Starting at the most basic level of survival.

So, think about this for a minute. A young female child who never experienced her basic survival needs of physiological, safety, belonging, and love by her father. It shouldn't come as a surprise that she's probably not going to have the greatest relationships with men. Because she was unable to rely on the man in her life, she became him.

In other words, because she could not trust and rely on the masculine in her life, she became the masculine that she could trust. She created within herself the very thing she needed to survive because she had no other choice. This level of survival can feel like life or death within the nervous system.

Basically, she became "the man", (not literally) because her childhood showed her that was the *only* way to survive, that was the only way for her to feel safe. And this becomes her normal operating system.

So fast forward to an adult, she has this protective armor on at all times (unknowingly and subconsciously).

Then she starts dating and she is this "strong and independent" woman and has an "I don't need a man" attitude. And because "she is the man" energetically… it's the vibe she sends out, no real "masculine men" are going to want to be with her, but she may attract more passive or feminized men.

It's not because she wants to be like this. It's exhausting, trust me, I've been there. She is just desperate to feel safe and trust in the masculine again. But old habits die hard.

So, when it comes to dating, she is carrying this vibe of *I don't need a man* because she has been her own rock for so long. But the catch is because she is radiating this tough energy, it's a bit of a repellent for real, solid guys. She's inadvertently sending out signals that say, "I'm the man here."

I hope this sheds some light on why things might be the way they are. It's a cycle that needs breaking, and the first step is awareness, understanding, and compassion and then the desire for things to change and doing whatever it takes to make those changes within each one of us.

Self-Sabotage, The Unexpected Talent We Have

So, why do women sometimes ruin relationships with good men? Why do men sometimes do the same thing? Why do any of us ruin a good thing?

Ever wonder about that?

Reflect back on your life, your past relationships, and your current relationships right now, and give it some actual thought.

Now ask yourself this question, "Where and how have I sabotaged good relationships in my life?"

This is not to beat yourself up. That's not the point here at all. Do not judge yourself here, just reflect. I have found within myself and my clients that if we are unwilling to see the truth within ourselves and our lives with who we are being and the choices we are making, we will be unable to create change.

Seven years ago, the bravest thing I ever did, was ask myself, what have I done to create the life that I am now living. Why do I keep choosing toxic men and then getting into relationships with them? Why do I keep settling for this? Why do I sabotage and ruin relationships with good men? Asking myself these questions and answering them rocked my world, it was like a smack across the face to *wake up*!

That's why I am asking you right now to consider these questions in your own life and in your own experiences. Without truly taking an honest look at yourself, your choices in life and then taking real ownership of them… there can be no change.

No matter what your story is, because let's be real, we have definitely become a society that *loves* to blame everything and everyone besides ourselves. We have definitely become victims in our own lives. And although you may get *all* kinds of attention for playing the victim, there is *no* power in that. There is *no* change in that, there is just more of the same poor-me story. The stories we tell ourselves dictate our whole reality.

And I can just hear some of you right now, you may think that is pretty cold, but it's not intended to be. I have deep compassion for your pain and suffering (I have experienced enough of it myself to last lifetimes, so I have deep empathy for you and it's part of the reason I do what I do and wrote this book).

But I also know that we can get stuck in the story, addicted to it even, allowing it to define us. And I also know *you* are powerful, so those things that brought you the pain and suffering are where your power lives. You are not your story.

Within the pain is the power. You can let it take you down or help you rise up. It can be the medicine or the poison. The gift or the curse. It's up to you how you choose to see it.

The most empowering thing I ever did when I asked myself those questions was to take radical responsibility for *my* actions, my choices, and my decisions in life. Sure, my exes were assholes, and they did some terrible things to me, but guess what? I am the one who chose them.

I allowed myself to be treated like that. *Me*. No one else. Only me. And I wasn't innocent, I was an asshole too.

So, take a good, honest look in the mirror, my friend. Who have you been in your relationships? Where have you deemed yourself unworthy of the kind of man or woman you deeply desire in your life?

Where have you sabotaged relationships with a great guy or an amazing woman?

I sabotaged relationships with great guys in the past and I knew why I did, I just couldn't stop myself from doing it (this is not a logical response, this is a nervous system response) because deep down I felt not good enough, that somehow he was better than me and that my greatest fear was that if I stayed in the relationship one day he would realize this truth that he was better than me (not actually true, but I believed it at the time) and he would find out who I really was (unworthy, not good enough, not deserving) and then dump me. So, I ruined it instead. I sabotaged it.

We ruin good things, and good relationships not as an intentional act of sabotage, not because we are crazy or stupid, although from the outside perspective that could be what it looks like.

It is an actual act of self-protection. Protecting yourself from past pain, disappointment, hurt, abandonment, etc.

We are hard-wired to survive at all costs and sometimes that relationship, that experience can feel like a saber-toothed tiger to us and to our nervous systems.

So sometimes we create protective shields around our hearts, or we numb ourselves out completely from feeling.

And the shield can make you feel so strong like no one can penetrate this shield. Yep, it certainly can serve greatly to protect you from pain.

But guess what? You also protect your heart from letting love in.

The very shield that you have created to protect yourself from pain is the same shield that will prevent you from experiencing the kind of deep, profound love you have always wanted and deserved.

I leave you with this to ponder. That "protector" that keeps you safe from the pain (and also the love) is in service to you, it is there to do the job of being your protector. So accept this, appreciate this part of you.

Ask yourself this question: What does that part of you, who is protecting you, want you to know? What is it trying to protect you from?

And then listen for the answer. Write it down, journal it, and allow whatever wants to come up to come up. You might be surprised at what is revealed to you.

Stop Treating Your Sex Life Like a To-Do List

Have you ever wondered why our romantic relationships' passion and fire sometimes go from sizzle to fizzle?

Many components can add to this dynamic such as a person's attachment styles, level of consciousness, unhealed childhood wounds, a person's life transitions (like recent divorce or parenthood), the phase of life they are in, etc. But what I see time and time again in my clients and in my own past relationships is that people just stop trying. They stop putting in the effort.

You stop making the relationship a priority and instead, it becomes this chore… this daunting job that you *have* to do.

It becomes part of your "To-Do" list:

Had sex with my partner. ☑

Got the groceries. ☑

Cleaned the house. ☑

Did homework with the kids. ☑

It loses its *pleasure* and *desire* and becomes part of your *obligations*; it becomes too much work. Nothing sexy or passionate about that. So how do you create and keep the sexy, the sizzle, the passion, the fire?

Here are some ways:

By making your relationship #1. ☑

Creating morning and bedtime rituals together to connect and reconnect. ☑

Spending time looking into each other's eyes close up (not staring). This can be challenging for different relationship attachment styles, but that's another conversation for a different book. ☑

Being each other's "go-to" person (not friends and not family, which can feel like betrayal to some). ☑

Tell each other things first, before you tell anyone else. ☑

Flirt, play, date, be adventurous, and have sex often. ☑

Take care of yourself. Make an effort to look good, smell good, feel good… be alluring. ☑

Do *not* talk negatively about them in front of them around others or behind their backs This one may seem like a no-brainer but you'd be surprised. I see this often when I first start to work with people and in my own past experiences I have had exes disrespect me to my face and behind my back, and I have also done the same and even though it would hurt, I wouldn't think anything of it because this was something I grew up seeing as "normal."

Bitching, complaining, and venting were just things that everyone did. Yet it is so disrespectful to your partner and your relationship and creates major resentment.

Create a "couple bubble" that encompasses some of the things I mentioned above, this includes making yourself a safe, no-judgment, fully accepting, and loving haven for your partner. This is part of the "specialness", the sacred bond that only you two share with each other.

There is more to this, but these are some that I see many miss or don't think about and they can make *all* the difference in the world.

Oh, and one more… put your damn phone down, turn the TV off and be *present* with him or her.

Be Your Real, Weird Self

Most dating advice sucks and doesn't work. So much of the dating advice out there is for you to literally change yourself to meet the desires or needs of someone else.

In essence: To change yourself to another version to somehow manipulate them into liking you. Yep, I used the word "manipulate", real talk here, as always.

Do you know what that message really says: *you as you are, is not good enough.*

So, because you are not good enough you need to change yourself to fit into someone else's mold of what they find to be "good enough" or worthy enough or attractive enough.

For a long time in my past, I believed that lie too. I had a belief that if I could just be whatever it was that someone else wanted me to be, I would somehow be lovable enough, I would be good enough.

And I became the best chameleon. I changed myself constantly to be whatever and whoever someone wanted me to be in order to be considered "good enough" to that person.

And this left me wondering after years of doing that, "Who *is* Melanie anyway?" I didn't even know who I was because I spent a large portion of my life being whatever anyone else needed me to be. Constantly seeking outside validation. Ouch.

But do you know what the truth was? That I could never be "good enough" for anyone until and unless I was "good enough" for me.

Dating advice and relationship advice are not different. The core message is: Change who you are to fit into what the current trend is for what guys like or what women like.

Be like this… don't be like that.

Say this… don't say that.

Do this… don't do that.

And the problem… who are you while you are following this advice to be *anyone* but you?

"Be a man, no, not like that, that's too much of a man, she will think you're a jerk."

"Be more feminine, no, not that, he'll think you're a slut."

"Pay for the meal, don't pay for the meal, get the door, don't get the door, don't call or text too soon, text right away, play hard to get, don't be too easy, be easy guys like that, they like when you chase, do this and it will make him want you more, do this and it will make her want you more." Blah, blah blah. It's all manipulation and playing games… *and* it's exhausting.

The best dating advice?

Hold on… are you ready? It's super simple… *Be the real you*, in *all* your quirky, weird, wonderful ways that make you uniquely *you*. That's the person you should be while dating and well, *all the time*.

And why would you want to be with someone who isn't attracted and enamored with who you really are anyway?

You can't possibly keep that charade up… eventually, all the parts of you that you have been trying so desperately to hide (because you were told it made you not good enough) are going to show themselves, and then what?

Well, you guessed it. You'll probably break up. Then declare: Next. Only to repeat this pattern again, unless, well… maybe this helped you to "see" differently. I hope so.

Be *you*. There is only one. None other exactly like you exists anywhere. Remember that.

And here's the thing… when you get "rejected" for being yourself, it hurts a whole lot less than being "rejected" when you weren't even being yourself to begin with. By the way, rejection is God's redirection.

To be *yourself* in a world that tells you to be anyone else takes courage and is the most beautiful thing you can do for yourself and for the world around you.

Why Good Men Might Seem Like Unicorns

Sis, you have been lied to about men.

If you are in a "not so hot" relationship or you can't seem to find any good men, sis, it's not your fault. You have been lied to. *We* have been lied to, not really in a malicious way, but nevertheless, somewhere we have learned that relationships are hard and that good men are hard to find. That you have to protect your heart at all costs because you don't want to get hurt.

We've been taught not to feel, to shut down our feelings and armor up. And no wonder, this world is a bit of a crazy place right now.

It definitely appears that good men are hard to find. Where did they go? Where did the "real" men go and why can't you seem to find one?

Why is dating so hard? And why do relationships seem to be such a challenge? Why can't you just find your "One" already, your soulmate, your forever partner, whatever you choose to call the true love you are seeking and deeply desire?

When did being a man start to involve vapes, porn, video games, work addiction, casual meaningless sex, lack of chivalry, inconsistency, saying he will do something yet doesn't, lacking leadership, doesn't protect you, being emotionally detached and shutdown, being too passive and allowing women to emasculate him or on the other side being abusive, controlling and dominant? P.S. Men: I am not bashing you. We need you. I have respect and love for men and with that being said, a lot of men have forgotten their true masculine essence and that is part of the problem.

Where did all the good men go?

Well, it's because, back to what I was saying before, you have been lied to. It's not your fault.

And you have also been a product of your environment, culture, childhood, religion, and gender. Basically, all the boxes society has placed you in that you unknowingly accepted as true. Again, Not. Your. Fault.

You see, we have this thing called our subconscious mind, maybe you've heard about it?

Maybe not. Either way, I'm going to share with you what it does and you'll soon understand why your struggles in love, dating, and relationships are what they are.

You see when we are little babies, young children, our subconscious minds are wide open and we literally absorb our environment as water absorbs into a sponge, and we become like this environment, the good, the bad, the right, the wrong, it all unconsciously becomes who we are. You could call it our personality if you want.

Well, at least for the time being, it becomes who we think we are. Think about it for a minute. Why do you think we are so similar to our parents' patterns, habits, and beliefs? Insert the "sponge," aka our subconscious mind. It's where the image we hold of ourselves is stored, our worthiness, what we think we deserve or don't deserve. Who we think we are.

As an example, if you grew up in a home where you were criticized often, then chances are you grew up feeling some lack of confidence in yourself, low self-esteem, and low self-worth. Maybe you were a people pleaser, an over-giver, or someone who had a hard time saying no.

Versus if you grew up in a peaceful home and you were praised and felt loved and accepted, then chances are you grew up feeling confident and strong and secure in yourself and your abilities.

This is part of what shapes us in our childhood and then becomes us as adults. Many adults are running around as children in adult bodies trying to get their needs met (that they never got in childhood from their parents or caretakers) within their romantic relationships.

Looking to get the love, affection, acceptance, and understanding that they never felt from their parents in a lover, and in a romantic partnership.

And when they don't get those unconscious/subconscious needs met they think there is something bad or wrong about that relationship or that partner and so they leave and move on to the next, looking for the person who will finally fill that void. That hole in their heart. Or, alternatively give up entirely, afraid to feel the heartache and disappointment again.

It's no wonder so many marriages end in divorce and why so many relationships fail. We are a bunch of little kids bleeding our childhood wounds all over our partners expecting them to love us and be to us what our caretakers never would or never were able to be.

It's not fair and not their job. And again, not your fault. You didn't know. You didn't learn these things in school. Your parents didn't know. No one teaches you this. But now you do know. So, the question is, what are you going to do about it?

You're Not Broken, Just Out of Stock

Do you have what it takes? The fact that you are here reading this book is the first and *most* important step and it means you have what it takes to create the relationships of your dreams; even if you have never seen hot, happy, and healthy relationships modeled, even if you have had a string of toxic relationships. Even if you have been divorced once, or twice, who's counting anyway?

Even if you think the word "true love" is a bunch of fairytale crap or maybe you have given up on love altogether, the fact that you are reading this book tells me that you have *exactly* what it takes to create the most epic, hot, loving, beautiful relationships.

The first thing I want you to know is that there is nothing wrong with you. You are not broken. You are good enough, worthy enough, deserving enough for the kind of relationships you truly desire.

Trust me, if I can do this (and I was a hot mess before), you can do this too. Attracting the kind of relationships you desire doesn't take as long as you think and it doesn't have to be as hard as you think.

Actually, you have what it takes *right now*.

If you have the desire for hotter, happier, and healthier relationships then you have exactly what it takes to get them. And guess what? It might even be easier than you think. You might even start to think, *How did I not know this??*

Before you beat yourself up for not knowing, remember it's not your fault because you did not know. You are probably wondering, *how did I not know this?* I think that by now the pieces are starting to come together and make sense and you're getting the picture.

So, what does it take to actually have a fulfilling sustainable loving, hot, happy, healthy relationships? What does it take to finally attract the *good* men, the *real* men, the hot masculine sexy men? The men who will finally treat you like the queen you are. And you might even be asking yourself, do you have what it takes to attract men like this, *kings*, as I like to call them?

That's the magic question that everyone wants to know, right?! *You* want to know. The short answer is *yes*, you do have what it takes *and* at the same time there is some tweaking that needs to happen, because let's face it, if you were 100% there, you would have him in your life right now.

I'm just keeping it real here as I always do. You didn't know any better before, but you are definitely getting the picture now, and *that* is worth celebrating!

Okay, so to get back to what it takes. The first thing is the awareness, the openness, the understanding that what you have done in the past in regards to your relationships is simply not working. Again, I'm not judging or blaming, just simply bringing awareness.

We cannot change *anything* in our lives if we are first, not made aware of its existence. We must first be willing to look in the mirror and be honest with ourselves.

How do you know that your relationships suck and that you want better if you were not aware that better exists, right? Awareness... that's first. Then do not accept the "norm" or what everyone else has so it should be "good enough" for you too. *Nope*, not anymore.

And then comes the drive, the will, the courage to *do* something about it. This can sometimes be the stickiest point for most people. To do whatever it takes. This is what separates people who have the most epic, incredible, beautiful, passionate next-level relationships from the mediocre ones, the kind that most people settle for.

They are willing to *do* whatever it takes and the funny thing is, well not funny ha-ha, but funny because it's absolutely silly and ridiculous that once you know, once you find out how you're going to be like WTF, *how and why didn't I know this? Why didn't someone teach this to me?* It's *sooooooo* simple. *Yet* so misunderstood.

I've been where you are, and I know the struggle is real. It's time to ditch the old stories that are holding you back. Trust me, I've seen the difference it can make.

Remember, you've got this.

Love Lies. Calling Bullshit on Dating Drama

Are you ready to ditch the old stories that may be keeping you from experiencing the kind of epic relationships you crave?

Let's slaughter some relationship myths, shall we? Here's the thing about today's modern relationships…

There's a common mindset around relationships and it is one of taking a "what have you done for me lately" kind of attitude, and it's not healthy. There is also a belief that relationships are hard. I'm not saying that it doesn't take a level of effort, but that does not mean it is hard.

Some also say that it's impossible to continue to have romance and passion long term. The "honeymoon phase," as they say is sure to fizzle out. Another myth.

Perhaps you've heard, or felt, that you are just doomed to have the typical boring relationship and you need to be realistic and settle down already. *I mean who do you think you are anyway?* Ha!

Have you heard this one before? "You need to lower your standards." Or these: *You are asking for too much,* or, *that kind of person does not exist* or *that relationship you want doesn't exist, you will never have it; that's some fairy tale make-believe lie.*

Then maybe you try harder, go on more dates, subscribe to more dating apps, swipe left and swipe right, only to be left feeling even more frustrated and annoyed… ugh… I know, right?! It's exhausting.

But, you keep going on dates, you keep putting yourself out there, you keep doing all the things they say. Who are *they* again anyway? I've often wondered this myself.

You keep doing all the things and trying harder and harder, maybe even listening to your friends and family's advice about what to do.

Perhaps even watch some YouTube videos on the subject. Basically, you keep doing the same thing over and over again and hoping *this* time it will be different. By the way, the definition of insanity is doing the same things over and over again and expecting different results. I am not calling you crazy, just thought I'd bring that to your attention.

Or maybe you have just given up completely. You are certain your man doesn't even exist and you remain single. After all, you are a strong, capable, self-sufficient woman. Who needs a man, right? Certainly not you. You can do everything on your own. Ha! Me too, I used to think and believe that myth too.

But do you really want to do everything on your own? Isn't it exhausting? Just because we can doesn't mean we should nor do we want to. I bet secretly or not so secretly, you deeply yearn for the day to be with the person who always has your back, who loves and accepts you for you. Someone who feels safe and a little dangerous (in the best possible ways if you know what I mean… wink wink). Do any of these thoughts sound familiar?

I have always said, that if you want to find "the one", you must first *be* "the one." This has nothing to do with being a "good woman." This has nothing to do with morality.

That's the thing most people don't get. And most don't teach. Why?

Well first, most don't know and we are conditioned to believe that the people we date, the people we get into relationships with, will be the ones who finally makes us happy.

We are taught that it is something to go get, to take from, to extract. We are taught to look for our other half, our better half, as we have often heard that expression, or this other myth from the movie Jerry Maguire, "You complete me." It's no wonder we are all confused when it comes to love, dating, and relationships.

How can you find, attract, and magnetize to you "the one" (the person you desire to have right now) when you do not have all those qualities you seek? And I'm not saying you are not. I don't actually know, but *you* do.

Having a beautiful, healthy, loving, passionate relationship is *not* about someone completing us. Although we have been told it is. It is not about getting something from someone.

How much can I take from this person or in my case, on the complete opposite side of that, I thought "If I just keep giving and giving, then eventually he will change" or "things will be different; he will see how great I am if I keep giving all of myself to this relationship," meanwhile expecting or getting very little in return. One-sided for sure. Have you ever told yourself those lies or something like that?

Here's a thought: If you want love, you must first be love and give love, and here's the real kicker: You do this without the whole attitude of "I'll *give* it after I *get* it first."

Not enough people talk about this. Very few speak the truth about why we struggle so much in love, dating, and relationships because quite frankly most do not actually know the truth themselves.

Not even the so-called experts. I made it my job to seek out the truth 7 years ago. After my second divorce, I felt deeply broken and ashamed for the "bad" choices I made. I was sure that there was something seriously wrong with me.

Furthermore, in seeking to fix my "brokenness," I became obsessed with uncovering the truth. I often thought: "This cannot be all there is, I cannot be doomed to walk in the same footprints as my mom, I will not get into one more toxic relationship."

This ends with me.

In my obsession with seeking the answers, seeking the truth and the wisdom that our ancient ancestors knew, I uncovered the secrets. With unwavering resolve, I became both investigator and test subject, embarking on a journey of self-experimentation.

When my life got dramatically different, as if I was a completely different person living in a completely different reality, I began attracting kings when I used to attract trolls.

I knew I had to teach this to the world; write books about it, like this one.

It's so much deeper than that. I felt deeply in my heart that it was and it *is* my duty and responsibility to share this with the world. It is my greatest gift, my passion, and my sacred purpose — for you, for me, for us.

Stop Being the Star in a Bad Relationship Reality Show

Here's the *real* reason you find yourself in a string of toxic relationships. I spent what seemed like the majority of my life wondering why I kept finding myself in unhealthy, aka toxic relationships. If this seems to be a similar reality for you too, you're going to want to read on.

So why is this? This used to frustrate me a lot and make me feel helpless all at the same time because deep down I felt the pain of being in a toxic relationship. It's not like I didn't know that it wasn't the healthiest of relationships, but at the same time, I didn't feel worthy of anything better and I didn't know why.

Sounds pretty messed up, I know. Have you ever felt this way in any of your relationships?

Unworthiness is something that can run deeply hidden within you. It's not this rational thought in your mind. It's not logical. And it's not a matter of common sense.

When we feel a deep sense of unworthiness in our relationships, we can end up going from one toxic relationship to another. Here are some of the reasons why:

- You felt unworthy of love as a child at some point, and/or at multiple points.
- You could have been told this or you could have just felt this.
- It can show up because you experienced your parents not being there for you emotionally or physically.
- It can show up because you felt abandoned by one or both of your parents, through divorce, separation, or work.

And so, where most people go wrong is that they end up going around in their relationships trying to "prove" their worthiness. They become hungry for that external validation that they didn't receive. Looking for that person who will *finally* make you feel worthy. It's an insatiable never-ending thirst.

Instead, try this:

For 1 day notice your "self-talk" as a non-biased observer. And write out what you notice. Try to remain non-judgmental of what you discover. If you are anything like who I used to be or who my clients are when they first start to work with me, your self-talk will probably be full of shit-talking and self-loathing. That's okay, we are simply observing.

Next, take the self-talk you have discovered and ask yourself if it is an actual fact (we are not talking about an opinion). Hint: it's not.

Lastly, change the self-talk to its opposite. Meaning, that if your self-talk is full of self-hate and self-loathing, change it to words of self-celebration and self-love. It can be helpful to think what would your best friend say about you?

Listen, I know how bad it sucks to go from one crappy relationship to another seeking to fill the void of unworthiness.

This is why I am so passionate about helping people kick their toxic relationships (and unworthiness) to the curb so that they can finally attract the love they desire.

Mirror, Mirror on the Wall

This is a truth that can be really hard to hear: Your relationships are a reflection of how you view yourself.

Eew, cringe. The good news? How you see yourself can change.

This is something I had to confront as I saw my mom's patterns of unhealthy relationships repeating themselves in my life.

If you're caught in patterns of codependency, conflict, competition, or emotional battles with loved ones. It says a lot about how you see yourself.

Do you tend to act as a chameleon, adapting to your partner's needs? You may have a pattern of putting others' needs above your own.

Always end up feeling like a doormat, used for others' advantage? You may have challenges with self-esteem.

Find yourself with partners who always seem aloof? You might be seeking validation from your partner.

Congrats! Noticing is the first step.

When I saw this in myself, I decided to wake up and *do* something about it. Once you identify how your self-image is playing into your relationship patterns, you can rewrite the script!

Take notice, and do some introspection. How do you see yourself?

What are your innermost beliefs and thoughts about yourself?

Keep the things, the characteristics you like, and change the ones you don't. Then rewrite *your* script; *your* story. Who do you want to be? How do you want to feel?

From Self-Hate to Self-Great

You've heard you've gotta love yourself first, right? But what does that even mean? The term "self-love" has become so overused, but there's so much value in it.

It means showing yourself affection and admiration. You know; admiring your strengths, reframing your shortcomings, respecting your body, forgiving your past, all that good stuff. One of the most important parts is overriding your self-talk. The stuff that goes on in your head and tells you, you suck.

Reinforcing your love for yourself automatically:

- Sets firm boundaries around how you allow yourself to be treated
- Gives you a sense of unrelenting regard for your worth
- Makes you feel secure being alone
- Allows you to show up as the invaluable being that you are
- Attracts an equal level of love and admiration to you
- You may have been looking for love in all the wrong places

It really starts on the inside. Maybe that sounds too easy or out of touch with reality, but there's nothing more effective than rewriting your programming around self-love.

Swipe Left on Insanity

I swear to God if I have to subscribe to another dating app, see another d!ck pic, or get ghosted one more time…

Woah, baby, let me stop you right there.

The way so many of us go about dating isn't working. I can see that. I've lived that. It makes you wonder if you should just settle for someone who's okay. It makes you doubt real love exists anymore. It's so exhausting to keep first-dating over and over again, hoping one of those matches will lead somewhere.

I know. I got sick of it too.

The crazy thing is you might even continue to do it over and over again, staying on the same hamster wheel and expecting a different result.

Telling yourself *this* time, it will be different, only for it to be the same, again and again, ugh.

You wanna know why?

Because *you* are the same, the way you think; the way you feel; what you believe to be true; and the actions you take are all the same.

Remember, "Insanity is doing the same thing over and over again and expecting different results."

The truth is, if you want different results, you have to be willing to do things differently.

Let's not sugarcoat it. *Different* results *do not* live in your comfort zone. I want you to understand right up front, that this can be so uncomfortable, especially in the beginning.

Let's be real, we have gotten way too complacent and comfortable as a society. I want to help you. I want you to do something that I have my clients do. Please try to do this from a place of a non-biased observer.

Try this for at least one day (*you can do it longer*):

Self-talk: notice how you talk to yourself throughout the day. Write it down, your inner speech and your outer speech.

Self-love: how do you care for yourself daily? What are you doing daily and consistently to "fill your own cup?"

Self-worth: how do you see yourself? Write out all the things you don't like about yourself and in a separate space write out all the things you do like about yourself. Compare. What did you notice?

No More Frogs

If you want to find "the one," you have to be "the one."

Your relationships are a direct reflection of your thoughts, feelings, and beliefs. Those unhealthy relationships are a result of poor thinking about yourself.

That realization, once fully understood and implemented, changed my relationships forever.

Here's a real example from my life:

Before: My (ex)husband would give me the silent treatment, call me names, talk down to me, and allow his family to get in the middle of our relationship.

Today: I would never allow that. Now, I would pay attention to red flags and I would hold my boundaries and create respect. I would never even entertain a relationship like that anymore. Now, I have beautiful relationships all around me, friends, family, clients, cool people to collaborate with, and dating kings when I used to attract trolls.

This can be true for you, too. If you want to sync up with your perfect match, you have to embody the attributes you need to have to attract that type of partner.

If you're still waiting for that Cinderella/Prince Charming moment, and settling for a relationship that's "good enough," this tactic won't work. Passively waiting and settling are surefire ways to block you from finding the love your heart truly desires.

While you're busy hooking up with people who aren't quite right for you, you might block your perfect partner from making a connection.

It's so easy to be complacent. It's so much easier than doing the internal work. But that's really what it takes to magnetize your dream partner, *the internal work*. It's always an inner game.

Here's the trick:

Write out the answer to these questions: How do I truly see myself? What is my current self-image? Your self-image is the beliefs you hold about yourself and changing it completely changes the kind of partners you attract.

To change those beliefs of what you can have, you have to rewrite a script. Write a paragraph about who you would have to be to attract and create the type of relationship that you really desire. What traits would you need to have?

Here's an example: I am so happy and grateful now that I am confident, fit, sexy, strong, loving, powerful, etc. It should be a paragraph that is descriptive of all the attributes that you want to embody.

As you write it, feel it to be true. You feel like it's done. The gratitude and appreciation of having it now. Go in your imagination and you see it, you feel it, you know it. You expect it to be true. It is done unto you.

So many people go in and out of relationships only to be left frustrated with why they keep attracting the "wrong" people and not knowing how to fix it and it doesn't have to be that way.

Try the things above and see how your relationships start to shift, but don't keep convincing yourself that it doesn't work with your expectation of more of the same crap you've always gotten. Keep your thoughts focused on the good that you desire.

Let Go and Let God

I have been brought to my knees more than once this year and many years before now, truly being what I felt was "forced" to give it all up to God, to take the burden from me, to surrender to the fact that no matter how hard I try, I can of mine own self do nothing. This does not mean I sit and meditate and do nothing, this means that I give it up to God and give thanks knowing that everything I need always comes and I listen to my intuition to be shown the way.

Keep Your Heart Open

We don't want to get hurt again, so we shut down, we shield ourselves from the pain, because at one point in our lives, we needed to, for our own survival, we felt unsafe otherwise. But then we end up carrying this shield around unknowingly, unconsciously to prevent that same pain, and at the same time keeping ourselves from feeling the very love we seek. But you are not the same person anymore. When we are living in a place of always being guarded from trying to feel the pain of the past, are we even living at all or are we merely existing? We want to feel all the "good stuff" but none of the "bad". Some of us want to feel all the bad stuff and none of the good because we feel we don't deserve it, but life is not made that way. If you are human, you are built to feel all of it, it's one of the most beautiful things about our humanity. It's in the pain *and* the pleasure that we appreciate all of life. I'm not saying it's always easy. I know it's not, but when we close our hearts to pain, we also close our hearts to love and truly living life in all its fullness.

Appreciate What's Good in Your Life Right Now

It's so easy to be negative and get sucked into all the things we are struggling with in life, I have been in many dark times in my life so I know how deep in pain and suffering we can get, but I have to remind myself often when that happens, *this too shall pass.*

Whether it is a great time or a horrible time in your life, the only time is actually right now, this very moment in each moment, and if we spend that moment hoping for a better moment, we miss the gift of this life altogether. Life is happening now and it's not on the other side of the career, the success the relationship, the divorce, the pain, or the happiness. It's right *now* and if you don't start paying attention you'll miss it.

Persistence is an Underrated Superpower

We are all so afraid to fail at something, but I know that if we *really* want something we will find a way. If we don't, we won't. If one way doesn't work, try another way. When things get hard it's easy to give up. At the same time, I find there is also a balance, a space between knowing when to give it up to God and knowing that God is the force behind your persistence, or when it's just your own stubborn nature of wanting to be right, or the fear running you, or judgment of others. I can't answer what that balance is for you, only you know that answer. How I find it myself is asking, what part of me is driving this ship? Is it my fears, is it my past, or is it what I know my heart and soul truly want no matter how scary? Is it that relentless push from within, my intuition that says keep going because it's the Truth or is it the inner critic within that tells you all the reasons why it won't work? At that point, I get quiet and listen for the answers.

The Unknown, Where All the Good Stuff is Hiding

We like to know what's going to happen. It's the part of our ego that needs certainty, and control, this part of us that thinks "Let me reason in my mind all the ways this could go bad or wrong so I can mentally prepare myself." It's all an illusion. The truth is, you don't know. The most beautiful ineffable experiences of my life have unfolded within the unknown, trusting in God the whole way, trusting that I don't need to know the how, in fact, I'm not the one in charge of how things will unfold, God is. My job is to trust, let go, and surrender and know the way will be revealed to me and I will know when it is time for me to know and not in my impatient time. It will be in God's time. *Thy* will be done, not mine.

Detach From the Outcome

Sometimes we want something so bad, that we create how the outcome needs to look in our minds, and when it doesn't go exactly to plan, we fall apart. Sometimes we have to just let go and accept things and people for exactly what and where they are and love them. It's a hard thing to do especially when you see so clearly what they do not, but it's not your job to convince anyone. We all have our own lives to lead and our own paths to walk and sometimes what people really need is for you just to accept them as they are, not fix, not save, but just simply be there and give them what they need, not what you think they need.

Give people the benefit of the doubt that they know what's best for them, just as you know what's best for you. We are all so quick to want to help and provide solutions for people and I think that's part of the beautiful hearts we have, but unless they hired you to be their coach they don't need to hear every opinion. We love to give unsolicited advice, but we forget to not see each other as helpless people who need to be rescued, but more so as powerful people whom maybe no one has seen or believed in that part of them. You can offer a different perspective, but ultimately, it's up to them what they do.

You Control Nothing but Yourself

As this world seems to be getting more and more insane, and upside down, so many people are losing faith, I have no doubt God always knows what to do, you don't create anything there ever was and anything that there ever will be and have no control over what is. God always has a plan, you may not know what it is or even be able to see it, in fact, we usually don't because our minds cannot fathom it, but if you could just hold the faith that everything will be ok, especially in the darkest of times and let go of the illusion of trying to control everything around you. Sometimes everything has to fall apart to be rebuilt and the only thing you actually can control is how you choose to see it... for you or against you, a gift or a curse. I always try to see the lesson in everything. What can I learn from this to be a better person?

Your Worth Can't Be Found in Any One Thing

Your value, your innate worthiness is not dependent on the money in your bank account, or in the number of clients you have or do not have, or in your trauma or not your trauma, or on the kind of car you drive or do not drive or house you live in, or in being single or in a relationship, or in any of your roles or titles, it cannot be found in any "thing" at all. The essence of your value is not located in anything, it just is. You are priceless.

Don't Forget Your Humanity

We have become so disconnected from each other, so easily dismissed or replaced with things, vices, objects, and "distractions" that we lack empathy and compassion and just overall kindness for each other, we are so worried about me and mine that we have forgotten our humanity and that we actually need each other. We weren't put on earth to be alone or do it all alone, although we have been sold the "lone wolf" mentality. The truth is, you never really know what someone is going through, maybe that nice little kind gesture you gave someone today meant the world to them and was the very thing they needed.

Your Body Keeps the Score

Our nervous systems are essential for our overall mental health and wellness and we are so out of touch with our body's wisdom and so in our heads that we pop pills, and consume drugs, alcohol, and porn. We numb ourselves out from the pain, we don't want to feel, and "feeling" is our nervous system so we dis-regulate and ignore it, numb it, only to end up having panic attacks, heart attacks, psychotic breaks, burnout, and dis-ease because we don't want to feel. When we don't want to feel, we can't listen to what our nervous systems need.

Occasionally we just need to chill out, and other times we need to express our anger in a healthy way. Sometimes it's rest and doing *nothing* and other times it's to do something… *anything*. Sometimes its spending time alone and getting quiet enough to hear what your intuition is telling you and sometimes it's being with the people who are good for our hearts and souls, sometimes it's forgiveness and acceptance of self, and other times it's forgiving others too. Talk nice to yourself, stop pushing so hard, and give yourself some grace, love, and kindness for once. You cannot give to others what you cannot first give to yourself.

The Dark Side of Feminism

Want to know where all the *good men* are? The good men of the world are under attack The dark side of feminism is contributing to this.

This is probably not common knowledge or a popular modern-day thought, but one thing you need to know about me is two important core values, which are authenticity and truth. We'd all be lying to ourselves if we didn't realize truly just how messed up our world is right now.

The world has flipped to what's good is bad and what's bad is good. It truly feels like we're living in the Twilight Zone. There are so many different levels of dysfunction going on in our world and one of them is the dark side of the feminist movement.

Yes, I know there was a lot of good that came out of it, but it has taken a dark turn recently. What I mean by this specifically right now is the injustice, the outrage that Good Men. *Good, Real Men,* men who are the way God made them to be are suffering! The real sad thing is that women won't realize it because men *are* so strong and they've been taught and conditioned to *not* show their feelings, to hide when they're in pain because it's weak... right?! Men have been hearing this mantra throughout their lives, "Suck it up" "Don't be a pussy" "Real men don't cry" all this crap! But the truth is, they do feel and that's a part of what makes them strong.

The thing that I want to talk about that is truth right now is specifically women who are using the fact that they are women to be vindictive, manipulative, and vengeful... to destroy good men.

Think about it this way...

Why do men go to jail when they don't pay child support, but women get put on welfare?

Why do men who are amazing loving fathers lose custody or not get custody or have a small percentage of custody of their children, when the mother is clearly not the nurturer or the better parent?

Why because she's a woman? And this is coming from a woman. I'm not saying this doesn't happen on the other side of the fence too. There is so much talk about the toxicity in men, but women can be just as toxic and, in many cases, way worse.

I'm sure you have heard the saying "Hell hath no fury like a woman scorned."

The "me too movement" is also a contributing factor, many women were honest and sincere and many were lying and up to no good.

And to be clear, there is *no* questioning that men are physically stronger than women.

But why are we not shining a light on women who falsely accuse men of sexual assault or physical assault and then get away with it because they're women?

Why are we not talking about women who actually are physically and verbally abusive to men… and they get away with it?

Because why? Many still believe women need to be rescued… the hero, knight in shining armor belief. "Oh, you poor little pathetic weak woman, this man is going to hurt you, so let us *save* you from this terrible man." Even though he was the *Good Man* in the relationship, and *she* was the abuser.

Do you know why? Because men don't talk about it. They just take it. They just take it over and over. And the sad thing is it is breaking them.

A good man can only take so much. He shouldn't have to take this.

Justice doesn't have a gender. What is right and what is wrong does not have a gender or skin color for that matter. It is about humanity. It is about the individual person and we need to stop putting our heads in the sand and act like everything is okay, when it isn't. Change happens when people have the courage to stand up and choose better.

I think the main reason our world is so turned upside down, so absolutely insane is because we have been doing that for *too* long.

We need to stop giving the stoplight to those who falsely claim victimhood while they're actually the ones perpetrating harm. You need to stand up for what the truth is in your life no matter if it's this or something else.

What's right is right. It doesn't matter if it's popular, and that is actually the hardest time to say it, with the stupid "cancel culture" that is in our society right now.

But guess what?! If you don't, if we don't, *nothing* is going to change. It's only going to get worse. If the good people of the world don't stop putting their heads in the sand and think these things will magically just go away and don't start *standing up* for what is right… for *truth*, the clowns of the circus are gonna take over… we're all gonna live in an insane asylum. It's time to wake up!

Maybe She's Not Too Much, Maybe You're Not Enough

Dear Men,

If you desire a truly feminine woman then you have to be willing to be a truly masculine man. WTF does that mean?! Hear me out…

I see so many men talking disrespectfully about how women are so masculine right now (boss babe) or she's too independent and she needs to submit to me. *I'm the man, she can never find a real man being that way.*

Okay, but let me ask you something, are *you* that masculine man?

Are you a safe space for her flow, her wildness, her fire, her power, her sensuality, her authenticity, her darkness and her light, her messiness, her wisdom, her gifts, her true essence or do you shut her down and try to control her because she is "too much?" No judgment, real question for you men, that requires you to be honest with yourself.

A woman who embodies her true femininity will "test" your ability to "handle all of her" (not in a manipulative way, it's her intuitive nature), and if you cannot lead her while holding the framework or container of which *all of her* can feel safe, seen, accepted, heard, loved, cherished and understood she cannot and will not submit, surrender, or whatever word you want to choose, to that man.

Her deep intuitive essence will not let her because she knows he is not safe and cannot be trusted.

Now this is not to take away women's own responsibility in healing their wounds with the masculine that can sometimes show up looking like mothering, controlling, and emasculating men. That is the responsibility of women, she cannot see you for the beautiful masculine king you are if she does not trust men.

But that's not your job to save or "fix" her, it's her work.

Know this... if you desire a more feminine woman, then *you* have to become the masculine man whom she would be magnetized to, who she deeply desires to surrender to, who she wants to unleash her fullest expression with and pour all of herself into deepest devotion to you.

There is way more to who this man is than the digits between his legs or in his bank account. Complaining and pointing the finger isn't going to get you there, it's time to look in the mirror and *rise*.

Your Battle Scars are Sexy

Dear Men,

Please don't give up. There are still good women out there, who will love you deeply and devotedly.

I know you have been hurt; you have the battle wounds on your heart to show for it. You have been mistreated, abused, neglected, discarded, demonized and emasculated. Injustices of the world have fallen on your shoulders and the weight has become unbearable.

Again, please don't give up.

She will not love you despite your past or your failures, she will love you even more *because* of them. She will honor and revere who you are

You are fully seen with her, loved, honored, accepted, respected, and appreciated for *all* that you are. She will nurture and nourish the little boy in you who never received the love and acceptance he needed and hold your heart with tenderness. But she will never treat you like a little boy.

She sees you the way God sees you, perfect, made in His image and likeness. She will give you perfect love. She sees her Divine King, God's selection for her, within you and she honors and respects the man you are

She has done the work to become the woman you deserve; she has gone through her own fires and has risen like the phoenix.

She is a warrior just like you and will be the greatest fan of your life, your biggest cheerleader.

Her appetite for you will be insatiable and she won't be able to get enough of you because it's so much more than sex, it's lovemaking in its purest rawest form… mind, body, heart, and soul in unison, as one.

Your love will release the wild in her, her true essence. She will soften and surrender unto you. She will trust your leadership.

This will be a love she always knew in her heart existed but never experienced. She will long for you and will gasp in your embrace.

She will honor your past pain, not out of pity, no, she will not love you despite your battle wounds. She will love you even more because of them. She sees you for the incredible man you are.

Her love is deep, there is no surface-level or superficial love here, only deep, loyal, devotional love. This love is unconditional. It is pure, sacred, holy, and rare. It doesn't compare or look for better. There is no "grass is greener" with this love. It is forever and it is only for *you*.

This is a love you may have never known, yet you have always deserved.

The Lie of Independence

Dear Women,

Drop your shield, drop your armor, remove your mask, society has lied to you, to me, to us.

We do need men. And they need us too, now more than ever. We can't do it all by ourselves, we're not meant to, this independent boss babe nonsense is a lie you have been sold to weaken us, to separate us, to divide us.

You are disconnected from your own feminine essence. Your radiance.

Women: this is not who you are, this is not real, you are not meant to be like this, this is not your Truth. Our bodies are tired because we have worn this wounded masculine shield for too long, we are getting sicker, and weaker, but we have been convinced that this is making us stronger. No, my sister, it is a lie.

You are made to receive, be in your body, nurture, love, create life, art, and businesses, and be in harmony with the rhythms of the Earth, the moon, with all of life.

You are meant to flow, to surrender, to move like water and fire, dance, create, and be the wise woman for your beloved, the oracle, side by side you are stronger, you are sovereign.

You do not need to protect your heart anymore. There are good men who will love you, protect you, cherish you, adore you, and lay down their life for you if necessary. They will not leave you for the next best thing, but you must put down your shield.

You cannot attract the good man you desire when you are carrying around this armor, guarded and afraid.

I know some men have hurt you in the past and you needed to protect your heart at all costs, but my sister, how is that working out for you today?

There are good men out there who will not hurt you, and who will love you, but you must keep your heart open to receive.

Trust, let go, and surrender into the unknown, knowing you are always on the right path, allow love, soften, open your heart, and do not give your power away anymore to what "they" tell you.

You are safe. Trust your discernment, you have learned your lessons, your intuition is your north star, always listen. It is God leading you always... you will never be led astray

Your mind will deceive you because it's trying to protect you from past pains... but how are you ever to receive love if you fear it?

The feminists have lied to us. The way we have been living is not what it is to be a woman, this is not the way God made you to be. Our ancient ancestors knew the way.

Allow me to remind you who you are. You are fierce, primal, passionate, sensual, beautiful, wild, and free, you are the light and the darkness and not in a way that society has told us that this darkness is evil, no, every life begins in the dark, from a seed to a baby, and within us we have to travel into our own darkness to come into the light.

You are the little girl, the maiden, the mother, the wise woman, and the *revered* one, *the crone*. You are Love.

You are infinitely wise, your intuition is your superpower, you are the protector in the spiritual realm for your beloved and your children, your family, you are magnetic and receptive (you were built to receive just look at your anatomy), soft, surrendered and vulnerable, no this does not make you weak, it makes you strong.

You are expressive and you speak your truth from a place of love that inspires and activates, it does not tear down, you are embodied, your temple is a wise and sacred vessel, you are open, flowing, caring, and kind.

You are also bold, audacious, fierce, powerful, sensual, and passionate.

Your grief is a superpower, do not hide your tears, weep for who you had to be so you can make space to rise into your power into who you really are.

You are divinity and humanity embodied, and it is time to remember that.

The Love That Changes Everything

The saying "opposites attract" isn't the way. The only thing that is opposite is your polarity, masculine and feminine.

The rest is a mirror. You will be very similar to your soulmate, hence the mirror, reflecting back to you, yourself. Complementary pairs.

Love is the greatest risk we will ever take. To be so open, raw, vulnerable, exposed, and "naked" — being able to open yourself. To be able to say, "This is me with all my imperfections, my good and my bad, my darkness and my light" is the most terrifying thought in the world to many of us. It brings up fear, death, loss, rejection, and betrayal.

We all say we want it, but many of us are deeply terrified of it. Very few people actually allow themselves to experience true, soulmate love. We love superficially and with conditions, that's not real love.

Instead, we wear masks and hide behind them thinking this will keep us safe. No, my love, it keeps you from experiencing the very thing you long for, the very thing you have always longed for.

Your true essence is love, it is the truth of who we are and our deepest space of evolution and growth, to transcend the consciousness of humanity, on this earth is to be initiated into this love.

This isn't a love you *find*. You must become it first and then it magnetizes to you. When you finally stop lying to yourself, shed the layers of lies you have taken on from this world and become your most authentic expression, the truth of who you uniquely are.

This is not a love that you have seen in movies, those are often wounded distortions of love. The love I speak of is a love created by God, the truth of love, unconditional love, devotional love, a sacred union between souls. True oneness.

It is the truth of who we are and why we are so deeply drawn to it. We are here to experience true love, to be loved, and to give love.

But you may not be able to enter into this union until you have purified yourself because you will not recognize its innocence, truth, purity, beauty, and rareness because you are still living in your wounded distortions and guarding your heart. It's here to initiate you into your deepest truth, your highest potential, your greatest expansion and to smack you awake.

This may feel uncomfortable at first if you've never known a love like this because it will bring up all the wounds of not having your needs met as a child that made you feel powerless, helpless, and afraid. We will tend to dissociate to protect ourselves from that pain. Deny it, run from it. Subconsciously, we vowed to never hurt like that again, so we put on the masks, adopted the lone wolf mentality, became hyper-independent, created separation, shut down our hearts, and convinced ourselves we are safer this way.

"I'll never be hurt by love again." This has become our comfort zone. It is a lie.

True love cannot be pushed or grasped for, only allowed and surrendered to by embodying pure love as deeply as you can.

This is the most important person you will ever meet. This love whispers. Let go, trust, and surrender into the unknown. I promise it will be better than you ever imagined.

When enough men and women come together in physical, loving, sexual, soulful union, and *merge*, the actual vibrational fabric of our reality will change. This is the greatest power.

That's why the inner work is paramount and why I am so passionate about it!

Unpack The Baggage You Didn't Know You Had

I believe the biggest challenges in relationships today come from unresolved childhood trauma.

Childhood trauma is not always abuse or something catastrophic. Sometimes it shows up as neglect, having to parent your parent, having to be a certain way so mom or dad don't get upset or mad (walking on eggshells), not having your mom, not having your dad, overly strict parents, emotionally unavailable parents, divorced parents, etc. Childhood trauma is basically, how the child felt within the circumstance or experience. How it is registered within their body is what constitutes it as trauma. It is deeply personal and unique to each of us.

This is not a blame game or shaming of parents, they did the best they could with what they knew. It's awareness. The way we can start to be better is by first becoming aware of where we are not. You can come from what society would refer to as a "normal family" and still experience trauma.

This is why we will do things like people-please, not speak up, become overly nice and passive, or really aggressive and explosive, try to save or fix people, give too much, lose our identities in relationships, turn into chameleons, become codependent, self-abandon or sabotage, have narcissistic tendencies, and get into abusive relationships.

This is not whether another person deems it as trauma, this is a very intimate and personal somatic (in the body) experience for that individual.

This is not something you simply "get over" or "time heals all wounds" these are unhealthy narratives, and you can't think your way out of it either. It's not logical or rational.

You know when people say, "Oh, get over it already, that was a long time ago. Why does this still bother you?" kind of stuff?

You cannot "get over" any kind of traumatic experience, you have to heal it at its source, at its root. So many people today are going in and out of relationships, some toxic, some healthy unconsciously seeking to heal from those childhood wounds, childhood traumas.

Picture this. A bunch of little children dressed up like adults, running around looking for the love, acceptance, and safety, that they never received from mom or dad in their adult romantic relationships. That's our modern dating and relationship world — only to keep attracting to them those wounds/traumas they need to heal and it's being shown to them as a mirror from the other person.

Because they are unaware of this unconscious program that is dictating every facet of their life (95% of every thought, feeling and action anyway) when they start to feel too much pain, that is what brings up the unconscious wounds/trauma of their childhood. Remember, they are not consciously aware of this, it is not in the thinking mind, this lives within the body, the nervous system, in our autopilot. This leads to usually pulling away and/or self-isolating and turning into the lone wolf. Swearing off relationships forever, or jumping into the next one right away. Anything to avoid feeling that pain ever again.

Understand this: you will continue to attract the same kind of person in a different body until you do the work to heal the parts that caused you to attract the "wrong ones" to begin with.

Also, on the occasion that you do attract a good man or a good woman, you will most likely sabotage it because you won't trust it and you will inevitably push them away or cause something to make them break up with you.

Because your nervous system doesn't know this feeling, we are subconsciously programmed to seek the "known" rather than the unknown.

The *unknown* feels like a threat, it registers as unsafe in your nervous system… *dangerous*. So, if what you have known is an unhealthy love, that's exactly what you will seek and what will feel comfortable until you do the work to heal it.

This is why you attract the "wrong person" — aka assholes, jerks, crazy bitches, gold diggers… you get the point.

The **known** can be pretty messed up. It is *so* important to understand that this is not logical. Again, this is why people who experienced parents or caretakers who were physically, sexually, emotionally abusive, alcoholics, drug users, narcissists, emotionally unavailable, cold, distant, critical, controlling, etc., will tend to seek (the *known*) partners who are similar to those caretakers.

The wonderful thing is, you can change it for good and have a beautiful, fulfilling life.

The Cosmic Joke

What if we looked at trauma or the terrible things that happened to us in a totally different light? What if we looked at all of our past "bad experiences" as something other than making us broken, messed up, or something to heal from?

I'm not denying there are parts of us that keep us stuck or repeating negative patterns that we have outgrown and definitely are not serving our greatest good. But once we get beyond that, what if the hypervigilance we had to create to survive gave us this incredible ability to scan a room and read people's intentions/energy?

What if the truth behind our people-pleasing is that we have a big, beautiful heart that is full of love?

What if we became an incredible parent that our kids get to have because we knew what it felt like not to have that?

What if that shame you felt around your sexuality was just to put you on the path to discovering the Truth of your wild and erotic sensual nature?

What if the negative talk that runs in your mind and tells you all the ways you suck and you're not good enough, was there to help you discover how to fall in love with yourself and discover just how magnificent you really are?

What if the people you attracted in your life with your romantic relationships were messengers to help you see within yourself all the ways you self-abandon and don't love yourself enough?

What if your greatest struggle that you have dealt with is your greatest contribution to the world, your magic, the gifts that you are here to share with the world?

What if it's all just this beautiful game and you are here to feel it *all*, to experience it *all*, the good, the bad, the happy, the sad, the heartbreak and the deepest love and everything in between... the ineffable totality of it *all* and that in this crazy, wild game of life, every single thing that happened brought you to the path to becoming your *self?*

What if it's Not Them, It's You?

It's not my fault. I wasn't the problem in the relationship. I'm a good person. I was a good husband, a good wife, a good partner… It's not me. It's them, they were the problem.

Have you ever said something like this before?

I used to think this too. And many of the times it is true for a lot of us. This is the common thought process for many people.

I don't need a coach, a therapist, a book, or any help because it's not my fault, they were the problem, I could see if it was my fault then yes, I would need that.

Nope. False.

Our nervous systems are formed a certain way. Our brains are wired a certain way, and our minds are developed in a certain way. They are formed within the womb, *but* even before that our DNA not only has the genetic codes that make us look like what we look like, but there are also thought patterns, beliefs, consciousness, and traumas that can come through our ancestral lineage. So, what is my point?

If you find yourself in a cycle of unhealthy toxic relationships it is absolutely your responsibility (not your fault, there is no judgment here) to end it, to do something about it, to heal, to be a better version of yourself because here's the deal:

- You are not your childhood
- You are not your past
- You are not your mother or your father
- You are not your failed relationships

But you are definitely 100% responsible for who you are and how you treat others in this world now.

If you don't like the kind of people you are attracting, if you find yourself frustrated in your relationships, stop pointing the finger at them and start looking in the mirror.

The most powerful revelation I had that changed the trajectory of my entire life for the better was asking myself, *What is wrong with you that you keep choosing these toxic men?*

I was the common denominator. I chose them. So, the question became what part of me chooses men like that? And why?

There was nothing inherently *wrong* with me, just like there is nothing *wrong* with you, but *something* definitely was wrong.

As adults, we are 100% responsible for our actions, and for who we are in this world and if you don't like who that is, then only you can do something about it.

It's not your fault until it is. At some point, you have to hold yourself accountable to be better. If you don't know how, there is no shame in that, in fact, it takes strength and courage to ask for help.

Until you can take a real, honest look at the reality of your contribution to your own relationship patterns, not just talk or complain about it, but actually *do* something about it, you will continue to attract the same person in a different body.

The Only Dating Tip You Will Ever Need

So, we all want better relationships, right?

Like who doesn't want to have more fun while we're dating and getting into relationships, but it definitely doesn't always feel like so much fun. In fact, it often feels maybe a little bit more like war. But here's the deal, this is the only thing you will ever need to know. You ready?

Do the inner work. Period.

- The answers aren't in this or that dating app.
- The answers aren't in getting advice from your friends or family who don't have the kind of relationships that you want.
- The answers aren't in *if I just go on enough dates, I'll find him or her*, aka a "numbers" game.
- The answers aren't in swearing off all men and women and remaining single because you are certain they suck and there are no good ones left.

You are seeking answers in the wrong place. It's within you. It always has been. You have just forgotten.

Do you want better relationships? Do you want to find the love of your life? Do you want better connections, deeper connections, sincere authentic, and healthy bonds in *all* of your relationships? Do the inner work to become it.

- Do the work to heal the parts of you that don't think you are worthy of love.
- Do the work to heal the parts of you who choose people who don't honor you.
- Do the work to heal the parts of you who still wear masks to fit in or hide.

- Do the work to heal the parts of you who abandons yourself to please others.
- Do the work to heal the parts of you that you have rejected or made out to be "wrong" or "bad".
- Do the work to heal the parts of you that wear armor around your heart.

Do the work to remember who you really are. You are a miracle and manifestation of God in human form here to experience the beauty, wonder, and awe that is *life* in all its flavors.

Boss Babe BS

Dear Men:

The feminists have lied to you. The modern boss babe movement is a lie too. Women don't want to do it all alone, all by themselves.

We love it when you court us, are romantic and chivalrous. We love it when you open doors and plan the dates. We love it when you open up your heart to us. We love the fierce warrior protector and the tender teddy bear heart you have for us.

We love how devoted you are to us. We love it when we can just let go and soften and know you got this; you got us. We appreciate and respect everything you do for us. We love all the intimacy and affection.

We love when you call us out on our BS in a loving way. We love how you always make us feel like the most important person in the world. We love how you take charge and take the lead. We love when you respectfully don't take our crap and have boundaries.

We love the good man, the God-man that you are. We love how deeply you love us.

None of us want to do this life alone, but the modern world has convinced us that we can, that we have to, or that we should, but it's a lie. It's to separate, divide, and conquer and many are falling for it. We were made for each other, so why are we fighting so much?

Why are we so at odds and in competition with each other? We crave union with you just as much as you do with us. It is our original design.

And this is important for you to know, the good woman who you deserve wants to give all of this back to you and more. Use your discernment to decipher.

Men's Silent Struggle

A heavy subject, one that I think doesn't get talked about enough and is of such importance, especially in these modern times. It's male suicide. Did you know that the leading cause of death in men under 50 is suicide?!

I don't pretend to have some magic solution, I really wish I did, but I do know after working with so many men over the years, being married to a couple, and raising two of them, many men do not feel safe sharing how they feel; to express their emotions, to cry, to be angry, to open their heart, to be vulnerable, and to be themselves.

And it's no wonder, we have lived in a world that has shamed men, made fun of men, criticized men for doing this, demonized and emasculated men. Men have been conditioned to hide how they feel., and it's killing them.

Maybe you've heard or even said things like this: *Don't be a pussy, what a little bitch, why are you crying, boys don't cry, men don't cry, suck it up, grow some balls, what a sissy, what a baby.*

So maybe you don't show how you feel because the world showed you that it wasn't safe. Instead, maybe you stuff it down and suffer in silence, all the while you put on a fake mask to conceal how you really feel so the people around you don't know.

Inside maybe you feel like you're dying, you hate yourself, you feel broken, you become depressed, anger would feel really good right now, but society has told you it's bad, it's toxic. By the way, it's not, it's normal and healthy, so instead you stuff it down again.

Maybe you drink, work even longer hours, take some pills, or do anything to numb. Anything to distract you from feeling the pain, the sadness, the emptiness. Maybe you suffer in silence, holding it all inside. Maybe things seem like they are too much, you can't bear it, and it gets real dark. I'm sorry the world has hurt you. I'm sorry it has not felt safe to be you.

Please, know that you matter. You are not alone, you are loved, you are seen, you are heard, you are safe, you are appreciated, you are valued, you are honored, your feelings, your heart, your emotions, your voice matters, how you feel matters. *You* matter. Especially if you don't hear those words or don't feel them to be true, they are.

You are so deserving of love, you were created out of love, from God. Please surround yourself with people who remind you of this. Please give this love to yourself always.

Your anger, your rage, your frustration, your sadness. *All* parts of you are sacred and beautiful. I know it may not feel like it, but this too shall pass, this feeling, this experience, I promise it will not last forever, hold on, please.

Don't take any of what I wrote the wrong way, I don't pretend to be a man, but I am a human, I feel as you feel, as we all feel, it is one of the most beautiful parts of being human, to feel and just as you may be feeling pain and sadness right now, please feel this love I am sending to you now.

The truth is none of us really know what is going on inside someone else, what they are dealing with, what they are going through. One needs to act accordingly.

We need to love each other more, we need more kindness with each other, more compassion, more connection, more respect, more appreciation, more understanding. We all need to be kinder, gentler, more forgiving, loving, and accepting of ourselves first and then each other because we cannot give to others what we don't have within ourselves.

Whether you realize this or not, we are all in this together.

Men Need TLC Too

Dear Women:

Our men are suffering.

They need our respect.

They need our appreciation.

They need our compassion.

They need our understanding.

They need our softness and peace.

They need our vulnerability.

They need us to need them.

They need to feel wanted and desired.

They need to be able to come home to peace, not more competition and conflict.

They need us to leave them alone sometimes and know that he will come to us when he is ready.

They need to know we love them no matter what

They need to know that it is safe to be themselves, it is safe to show and express how they really feel.

They need our love.

They need to be valued.

They need our support, adoration, and devotion.

He does not need you to be his mother.

He does not need you to criticize or control him or tell him what to do and how to do it.

This emasculates him and will never make him the man he was born to be.

In fact, this will make him resent you, close his heart off to you, and bring out the worst in him.

If you want the best out of him… if you want a good man… then you must *see* the *best* in men.

Explode The Box

Less self-criticism and more self-acceptance.

Less selflessness and more selfishness (fill up your cup first).

Less self-loathing and more self-loving.

Less people-pleasing and more pleasing yourself.

Less caring about what others think of you and more caring about what you think of you.

Less listening to your head and more listening to your intuition.

Less trying to prove your worth and more accepting that you are God's highest creation and have always been worthy.

Less giving away your power and more standing in your power.

Less looking for the bad and more looking for the good.

`Less making decisions out of fear and more making decisions out of love.

Less living within all the boxes society has put you in and more exploding those boxes.

Less waiting for conditions to be perfect for you to be happy and more choosing to be happy now.

Less trying to control everything around you and more surrendering to the beauty of letting go and knowing everything will work out for the best.

Less shutting your mouth because it's easier and more speaking what's on your heart from a place of love because it's true.

Less being who everyone else thinks you should be and more being who you want to be.

Less keeping yourself small and more being audacious, big, and bold.

Less judging of others and more taking responsibility for self.

Less looking out "there" and more introspection and looking inside of you.

Less trying to find the one and more being the one.

Less doing and more being.

Less living your life for others and more living your life for yourself.

Less settling for what you think you can have and more expanding and growing beyond your wildest dreams.

Less being realistic and more understanding that you are the creator of your reality so go ahead and be delusional.

Less loving people with conditions and more unconditional love.

Less doing what's comfortable and more expanding into the unknown.

Less expecting the worst and more expecting the best.

Less protection and guarding of the heart and more openness and expansion of the heart.

Less disconnected casual sex and more uninhibited mind-blowing transcendent lovemaking.

Less bitching and complaining and more appreciation.

Less calibrating to others' expectations of you and more calibrating to your own.

Less fakeness and more authenticity.

Less toxic relationships and more healthy relationships.

Less blaming others for your unhappiness and more taking accountability and responsibility for your choices that led you to be unhappy.

Less telling people what they want to hear and more telling them what they need to hear, especially yourself.

Less telling other people how to live their lives and more living your own.

Less criticizing others and more uplifting others.

Less feeling bad and more feeling good.

Less focus on all the things you don't want and more focus on all the things you do want.

Less seriousness and more playfulness and fun.

Less numbing out and more feeling it all.

Less beating yourself up for past mistakes and more acceptance that you did the best you could at the time.

Less staying stuck in your unhealthy choices and more doing whatever it takes to work through it.

Less being nonchalant in your relationships and more being *all in*.

Less choosing others and more choosing yourself.

Less running your life on what you "should do" and more choosing to do the things that light you up.

Less "normal" relationships and more hot, happy, and healthy relationships.

No More Mr. Nice Guy

Dear Men:

It was never your job to save her.

It was never your job to take her disrespect.

If you desire a feminine woman you are going to have to stop believing "them."

You will have to stop being the "nice guy."

You will have to stop being the pushover.

You will have to stop worrying about what "they" think.

And you will have to stop letting her control you and "wear the pants."

You will have to stop letting her criticize you and have boundaries.

And you will have to start being the true man God made you to be.

If you want a more feminine woman, *be* a more masculine man.

A woman doesn't want to wear the pants, tell you what to do, and lead in the relationship, but she will if she has to.

Don't point the finger at her and tell her all the ways she needs to stop being so bossy.

Don't point your finger at her telling her all the ways she needs to stop being so controlling.

When did you become so passive?

Point your finger at yourself and become the man who leads by example.

Point your finger at yourself and ask, when did you forget who you were?

When did you stop respecting and loving yourself?

When did you forget your power?

If you want her to be softer, surrendered and in her authentic feminine nature be the man she feels safe enough to do that with.

This does not take away her responsibility to become receptive to your masculinity; you cannot rescue or save her enough to ever make that happen. That is her work and her work alone.

In a world that makes it easy to blame others, *be* the one who looks in the mirror and takes responsibility for how you got to where you are in the first place, and then be courageous enough to be the incredible man God made you to be. I promise you'll become irresistible to true feminine women.

WTF

Sometimes life kicks you in the ass to wake you up to yourself. Sometimes the "bad" things that happen to us are there as catalysts for us to heal the relationship we have with ourselves.

I remember being on my knees praying to God while I was going through my first divorce while my ex was making it his mission to destroy me, to break me and the depth of hate he had for me is more than words can express. It first started financially and when that didn't work, he started to turn my kids against me at all costs, they were his weapon of choice, never mind what it did to them.

There I was begging for mercy saying to God, "Why are you doing this to me?" I felt within every ounce of my being that I was being punished for a crime I did not commit.

It was a very dark time, one of the hardest of my life, and because I was stubborn, I would not allow any of the things he was doing to destroy me. In fact, it taught me some of the greatest lessons.

I was never being punished. God doesn't punish you or me. God is the purest form of unconditional love. You, me, all of us are extensions of God. I wasn't being punished, I was being smacked awake to all the ways I lied to myself, to all the ways I hated myself, to all the ways I made stories about how I was not good enough or worthy enough or educated enough or came from a good enough family, too broken, I could go on and on. I think you get it.

Here are some of the incorrect beliefs I used to have about myself a long time ago. Maybe you've believed them too for yourself:

I come from a broken home, multiple divorces so no one good or educated or wonderful will want me.

I have to prove that I am good enough or they won't love me or accept me and they'll leave.

I grew up in a lower middle class, with not a lot of money, no one graduated college in my family so no one educated or successful will want me.

I need to choose the guy who pays the most attention to me because he must really love me; and because I am so unlovable I just need to take what I can get.

My dad left when I was little and had many stepdads who just kept leaving, so that must mean I am not worthy of love, there must be something wrong with me if they keep leaving.

Crying makes me weak. I will never show my tears.

Vulnerability is a sign of weakness, no one will ever see that side of me.

I must change myself into what "they" want me to be in order to be loved.

My mom was pathetic because she depended on men, that will never be me. I will always take care of myself, I don't need, a man. They will leave anyway.

My needs don't matter so there is no point in saying what I want because no one cares anyway.

Do any of those sound familiar to you? The dysfunctional experiences I have gone through in my life brought me to all the places inside of me that I had forsaken.

I have a beautiful life because I did the inner work to create it. I cried, I felt all my shame, my guilt, my fear, my rage, my grief, my betrayal. I felt *it all*. And then I felt good again. Basically, releasing all the lies I have thought and believed over the years. By releasing the emotion, you release the energy around it. Ever notice how you feel better after a good cry? That's why.

And I got help. I did not do this alone. The people around me were just as clueless as I was. I needed professionals, mentors, and role models who walked the walk. Asking for help is never a weakness, it has always been a strength, we have just been collectively taught the opposite.

In that, I found acceptance of myself, forgiveness for me, understanding for me, compassion for me, and love for me. I was never ever broken or bad and neither are you.

In feeling there is healing. Don't be afraid, don't suppress it anymore. You liberate yourself when you give yourself permission to be with whatever is there.

I share this with you to show you how we can make stories up in our minds that make us so wrong and so bad and so unworthy that it can and it will wreak havoc in your life, but *only* if you let it. If you believe it, you perpetuate the cycle of it showing up in your life. If you let it in, all of that falling apart around you, you find *yourself.*

You have to find the real *you*, the you who God made you to be. The you under all the lies you unknowingly took on as truth about yourself. It's like a great unbecoming to become all that you truly are.

I see *you*, the beautiful, wonderful, joyful, excited, fun-loving incredible *self* that you came here to be.

The Real Man Manifesto

Dear Women:

Do you ever ask yourself, where are all the "real men"? Where are all the good men? Where are all the masculine men who plan the date, open the door, and treat you like a queen?

The ones that you feel safe around, protected, not just physically but also in your heart. The ones who are true partners on the team of "us" and "we" so you never have to do it all alone again. The ones who know what they want, who they are, and are clear, decisive, and go after what they want, including and especially *you*.

The ones who do not play games, vape or are addicted to porn and would rather hang out with the "boys" instead of you. The ones who will always let you know exactly where you stand and never have you second guess their intentions with you.

The ones who make your relationship a priority and will ravish you with a passion that leaves you breathless and craving more. The ones who pursue you — you will never have to chase a "real man." The ones you can finally let your guard down with and soften into your true feminine essence. Do you want to know where they are?

They are all around you. You just might be unknowingly repelling them instead of magnetizing them to you.

Question your beliefs about men.

Do you believe there are no good ones left? Then that's what you will get, no good ones. Do you believe they are all cheating jerks? Then that's what you will get, cheating jerks.

It's actually quite simple when you understand it. You, we, all of us are co-creators with God of our own little world within this great big world. If you don't like what you are seeing, or what you are getting, then only you can change that. And you change that by what you focus on. Don't think there are any good men left? Tell yourself the opposite until you believe it. It's not seeing is believing, it's when you believe it, that you will have the eyes to "see" it.

The Ugly Truth

Dear Women:

If you are one of the women who is having a hard time finding a good man. Here is a dose of perhaps the real reason you can't seem to find one. It is because deep down, you either hate, dislike, or don't trust men or you don't believe "good men" exist, or at least not the kind you want. Or you don't feel worthy or deserving of that kind of man.

It is as simple as that. Now changing that belief, is usually not so simple.

I can hear you now, "But it's true! I feel this way because of my own experiences with men."

And my question to you is, how's that "truth" working out for you? Not so good I'll bet. Change your perception. Question your beliefs. I know for a fact there are plenty of wonderful men, just like there are plenty of wonderful women. But your consistent thinking and believing that there isn't is the very thing that keeps you from what it is that you want: a plethora of good men and women to date and to choose from. Stop buying into what "they" say. What do you want? And concentrate on that.

You Need to Own It

Instead of getting closer as men and women, we seem to be getting further and further apart. There is a lot of detest and resentment towards each other, as well as blame and shame.

Here's the thing I want you to know before you complain about how bad women are or how bad men are. I want you to take a look in the mirror because it's easy to point out others flaws or where they screwed up, right?

But what about you? Where did you drop the ball? How could you have shown up better? What did you do to make their lives better or easier? Would you date you or marry you?

How did you treat their friends or family? Were you there for them when they needed you? Did you feel safe, seen, and heard? — and did you allow them to be safe, seen, and heard?

Was it a team effort? Did you try to fix or save them and then end up resenting them because they didn't change into the potential you fell for? Were you loving and accepting of them exactly as they are? — or did you criticize or control?

Did you manipulate or use things against them? Did you fight to win the argument or did you listen to understand? Did you treat them with respect and kindness?

Did you go out of your way to show them that you care? Did you make them and your relationship a priority? Did you take too much crap and not speak up for yourself? Did you make yourself into who you thought they would like instead of showing them the real you?

Did you shut down and give up and stop trying? Did you stop having sex?

Did you love them so much that you put them on a pedestal and forgot how to love yourself too? Was there giving and receiving between both of you or was it more one-sided?

There are so many questions I could ask you. But the *best* thing you can do for yourself and your future partner is check yourself. Own your part. Take responsibility and accountability for how *you* showed up or didn't in the relationship and then do the work to become better.

No one is perfect, we all have our so-called flaws but pointing your finger at someone else who you think did you wrong is not going to change anything in your life. It's only going to make you bitter, jaded, and resentful in the end. Instead of being happy, you'll probably end up miserable.

Ask yourself: What part of you chooses that kind of unhealthy, toxic, or not-so-great partner? Or what part of you *is* that partner?

That's the real question — and not to condemn yourself or make yourself wrong or bad, but to look at the truth of who you are being or who you have been.

Blame can feel good at times, but there is *no power* in that. You cannot change how anyone else shows up and you do not and cannot control them.

But you can change how you show up and that's where *all* the power is.

Freaky Fabulous

All women want a "good guy" in the world and a "bad boy" in the bedroom.

There are parts of ourselves that we often neglect, push down, and suppress that we actually need the most love and compassion for. The parts of you that you were made fun of, yelled at for, shamed for, made to feel bad or wrong for, or embarrassed of, criticized for; the unlovable parts, the unworthy parts, the despicable parts the parts that you want so desperately to hide from everyone including yourself. The parts that you don't want anyone to know about or see. The parts that would leave you feeling unsafe, cracked wide open, exposed, vulnerable, raw, naked.

If anyone knew about them you would soon rather die or hide yourself forever. The parts you stuff down, repress, or numb yourself out from feeling. It might even make you uncomfortable just to think about it as you're reading this. Yes, those parts right there.

The ones that hurt us when we were a child and often we don't recall parts of our childhood because of this (and sometimes later in life too.) Those are the parts that need your love, understanding, acceptance, and validation the *most*.

Those are the parts that need healing and to be felt and to feel safe exactly as is, there is nothing to "get rid of."

It's easy to like the so-called "good" in ourselves and others, — the *light*. It's not so easy to like the *bad or the wrong* — the "darkness" (darkness does not mean evil).

By the way, "good and bad" are just labels we like to label people (ourselves included) in boxes because it makes us feel safe.

There was never anything wrong with your so-called dark or bad parts. You just had people in your life who didn't recognize their own divinity, their own goodness, and they were not emotionally regulated, so how could they help you see yours?

The human that is you is the light and the dark. Think of it as a flower or a tree that has deep roots in the earth (darkness) and then it grows into the light and it is both, the dark and the light.

You were never broken, you just felt like you were, there is no part of you that you ever needed to "get rid of." If you cannot accept and love yourself for all that you are, you cannot ever do the same for another.

It is the core of where all judgment comes from and the truth is we have gotten really good at judging and condemning ourselves and others. You can never "cut off" any part of yourself and feel whole. Your darkness is the key to your light.

Everything that is holding you back is in discovering the darkest parts of you. You must understand it was never bad, it was just misunderstood.

First, you find your light, then you find your darkness, then you find yourself.

Dear Knight in Shining Armor

It's not your job to rescue her

She doesn't need to be saved

She's not yours to save anyway

That's not your job, it's hers

You don't need to be the knight in shining armor

You don't have to fix her daddy issues

You can't actually

She was never broken

You don't have to tolerate her abuse

It doesn't make you a failure if you leave or if she does

It doesn't make you less of a man if you cry, it takes courage to feel deeply

Your job was never to save the world

Only to save or become yourself

The world's burdens are not yours to carry

Let them go, they are too heavy

All the pain you have experienced was never a punishment

Sometimes you have to go into your darkness to realize you have always been the light.

You were always worthy of a perfect love, you just had to find it in yourself first. The healthy loving relationship you want requires mastery of being good with being alone first.

God's Whisper vs. The Shit-Talker

Your intuition is your superpower. It is God talking to you. Listen to it *always*. It is never wrong. It is always right. It will always lead you down the right path, your perfect path.

Many people don't trust their intuition because they don't trust themselves, that used to be me too. And let me tell you, when I ignored my intuition, I suffered the consequences.

Sometimes we don't even know how to tell the difference with all the thoughts that run around in our heads. That's because the shit talker (what I like to refer to as what you may call your inner critic) runs amuck in our heads telling us all the ways we suck, and that voice can be really loud.

Here's how I have deciphered the two:

In every moment there are two thoughts or voices. Well, there's more, but just stay with me. Your intuition is always first, but initially, that inner critic is the loudest, so pay attention.

Your intuition is first and can sometimes sound like a whisper, it can come to you as a hunch, as a vision, as a flash, as an inner knowing, as a feeling of "I know that I know that I know, I cannot explain why, I just know," in other words, inner knowing without explanation.

It can come to you as a random thought, as words on a page, or as a picture. As a voice that says to turn left, when you were supposed to go straight.

Sometimes it comes as a feeling that comes over you, as a compulsion or a pull towards someone or to do something. These are some of the ways.

It cannot be explained and is not to be reasoned with. It just is. It simply points the way. And if it does come with a "feeling," that feeling is always positive or it is neutral, and it is often not "logical." It never ever has a negative feeling or thought associated with it.

If you feel negativity, it is your trauma; your past, your fears, your worries, your doubts, and your triggers. In other words, the things you have not dealt with yet, that inner critic starts off way louder than your intuition, that's why we listen to it at first.

It will try to reason with you as to why whatever it is that your intuition told you to do is a bad idea because sometimes our intuition makes no sense, and because we are logical, we want to make sense of things. Alternatively, our intuition often does not make sense, it is often not "logical" and our reasoning mind can't understand, especially since the shit talker is mostly based on our past experiences to try to prevent us from getting hurt again.

Because at our primal core, we are built to survive, "not to die" so to speak, that pain that you experienced from that last relationship, that heartbreak registers to the shit talker as "dying," so it's going to convince you all the reasons why this new romantic partner in your life is going to hurt you just like the last one. These are thoughts to keep you "safe", but in this case, safe only means not repeating the same pattern, it doesn't equate to actual safety, you were never in danger of any death.

So, in its protection from past pain ("dying"), it prevents you from the happiness and the love you seek if you listen to it.

That inner critic will sound logical, and reasonable, and you will often think, yes that makes sense and then you will create an argument within yourself to listen to the shit-talker instead of your intuition. Bad idea.

Again, your intuition is God leading you down your perfect path. The Divine plan. It's not always an easy path, but I promise you it's your path to greatness, to having your desires.

To help you tune more into your own intuition, I suggest a few different things: get quiet in your own thoughts, get out in nature, meditate, pray, and spend time in silence and introspection. Cut out the noise and distractions of our busy world, like TV, phones, and others. This will help you tune in even more to be able to hear your intuition, your inner knowing, and God's guidance.

Permission To Be a Jerk

For some people, and I know this was me, at the beginning of healing and unbecoming, in the unlearning, is that sometimes being "nice" is the last thing you need to be.

Sometimes being a jerk is what you need to be. Temporarily. We live in what feels like crazy cruel times, and because of that I hear a lot of people telling everyone to be kind and nice and for the most part, I do agree. But, sometimes for a moment in time, being nice is *not* the answer.

If you grew up in an environment where you were the nice one, the kind one, the good little boy, the good little girl, the nice guy, in other words, you did what you were told. You did the "right thing", you were the "better person", you took the "high road", you were "good", and didn't want to make anyone else feel bad or hurt anyone's feelings. You often sucked it up and bit your tongue, you became a people pleaser. Then somewhere along the line people took advantage of your kindness. People took you for granted and used you, manipulated you, hurt you, used your kindness against you, disrespected you, and mistreated you. They mistook your kindness for weakness.

If anything like that was your experience, the last thing you need right now to be is nice! Your anger is sacred. Your rage is sacred. And you have the right to feel it.

What you really need, your medicine right now, is to let it out in a healthy way. Express it! No more suppressing it and holding it in.

Tell the people in your life who have treated you badly and I don't care if it's your mom, your dad, your aunt, your grandpa, your sibling, or your neighbor. I don't care who it is. Tell them how you really feel. Let them know all the ways they hurt you and how you are no longer going to tolerate it, so they can either step up and treat you with the kindness and respect you deserve or they can get out. You must stop sucking it up and silencing your voice and telling yourself you're doing the "right thing" because you are not. You are letting fear dictate your life and it's causing you to lose respect for yourself. Stop lying to yourself, it doesn't make you "good," it makes you a doormat.

When you have spent a lifetime being "good" what you really need for a moment in time is permission to be "bad." So, here's your permission. Tell people to mind their own business and to stop telling you what to do, how to do it, or how to be.

Don't worry, you won't stay "here", in this anger for long, you'll let it out, you'll release all that pent-up poison you have been holding onto, and then you will probably feel like an elephant just jumped off your back.

They may not like it at first, but they will have way more respect for you and treat you better. This is an act of self-love. This is an act of self-respect and courage.

Whatever it is you need to say, whatever you have been wanting to say, say it. This is why we sometimes feel like crap like something is wrong or broken or we need to fix it.

It's your soul saying, stop betraying yourself. *You* are important also, you matter too. If you keep holding it in, you're going to get sick and depressed and it can turn into disease.

Anger expressed is healthy, all emotions expressed in the moment are healthy. It's the suppression that leads to many unwanted things like what I mentioned above. Not everyone deserves your kindness. Sometimes people deserve your wrath, at least temporarily.

This is how you start to respect yourself again and how you take back your power. This is how you start to feel good again.

Even Jesus Got Pissed

If you really want to take it to another level about allowing yourself to be fully expressed, here's more inspiration: Even Jesus got angry and flipped over tables.

Our society has forgotten its humanness. That's because for so long we have been made to feel bad or wrong to express or show how we feel.

Have you ever heard phrases like these? *Stop crying or I'll give you something to cry about. What a crybaby…*

Some people would rather see you on antidepressants and sad than let out your anger. As a nation we are so dysregulated in our nervous systems because we don't express our emotions, instead we suppress our emotions. To feel is human, and to allow ourselves to express those emotions is human. When we don't, we do things like get sick, diseased, marry the wrong people, and stay in terrible relationships.

It is because we don't listen to our bodies that we have gotten so conditioned to not feel, that we become numb, as we keep stuffing it down and eventually the body will have enough. The body is the ultimate scorekeeper. So, you have to let it out and sometimes letting it out comes in the words you speak.

In a society that has encouraged us to numb out, stuff down, and be afraid, you dare to feel. It is part of your humanity. It does not make you bad, wrong, or weak. It makes you a human being who is born to feel it all.

The only problem with feeling big feelings, and uncomfortable feelings is the story we tell ourselves about what it means.

Stop the story that means that there is anything wrong with you and start telling yourself the story that it's ok, give yourself permission, say "I am safe and everything will work itself out." Love the hell out of yourself during those times, accept this just is what it is right now and it doesn't have to mean anything and it's not going to last forever

When we are feeling uncomfortable feelings, for all of us this can be different. Uncomfortable, simply put, means feelings that you are not used to feeling. For some it is anger, for others it is love, for some it is fear, for others it is pleasure. Whatever it is for you, feel it, breathe into the discomfort, be in your body, quiet the noise the mind is making, feel the love and acceptance for yourself at that moment, and say things like "I am ok, I am safe, there is nothing for me to do right now." Take deep breaths and allow your nervous system to relax.

In a world that wants you sick, on meds, numbed out, stressed out, overworked, and riddled with fear so you are easy to control, have the courage to lean into your humanity and feel — especially those uncomfortable emotions. Give yourself all the love, understanding, validation, and acknowledgment in those moments, and watch just how much freer and fuller of life you start to become.

The Real Cost of Dating

Dear Men:

I wonder if you've ever considered this: What's more expensive?

Continuing to take women on dates, paying to romance them, paying to wine and dine them, and then get into a relationship with one of those women, only to discover down the road (sometimes months, usually years) that she's just like all the other "wrong ones."

I wonder how much that costs? Probably *a lot*. Which then leads you to more frustration, aggravation, and ultimately misery. Have you ever considered what is the price of your mental health and well-being? And, or you get married and find yourself in a costly divorce. By the way, they are *all* costly mentally and financially. Maybe it's not your first one. How much is your monthly alimony and/or child support obligation?

Or…

You do the inner work to finally get to the root cause, the real issues, the unaddressed unconscious beliefs and patterns within your mind and body that prohibit you from the love and life you want.

The right partner is out there, and the journey to find her starts with making the right decision now, not tomorrow or Monday, because that day will never come.

When you change your approach, you change your life.

Wounded Warrior

Dear Men:

I know you have been hurt too. I see your pain even when you try to hide it. Your strength, love, kindness, courage, and masculinity have been used against you as a weapon. You have been under attack without even realizing it sometimes. It has shown up in places you never thought possible.

Wounds that burden you with shame, guilt, anger, resentment, and self-loathing. Wounds that you did nothing to deserve, yet here you are cut open. Wounds from the women in your life, the feminine. These wounds could come from any woman in your life. Sometimes it's your mother, your sister, your grandmother, your friend, your lover, your wife, or your ex.

This is not to condemn them either or make them wrong, most of them have unconsciously hurt you. But knowing that maybe they didn't mean to hurt you, and although some did, it does nothing to remove the pain you feel, as well as the scar on your heart that remains.

Here are some ways that a wound around the feminine can show up in your life:

- Over giving in your relationships, one-sidedness
- Feeling the need to rescue, save or come in as the "white knight"
- Attracting women with daddy issues or who need you to save them from their boyfriend, husband, or father
- Getting into relationships with women who control and criticize you, talk down to you, and make you feel like you can't do anything right
- Guarding your heart and scared to death of choosing the "wrong one" again, so you do nothing instead
- Hating on women and condemning them, thinking all women are "the same" as the ones who hurt you

- Having an attitude that women are sluts, gold diggers, bad, evil, no good ones left
- Easily manipulated by women with tears or emotion
- A need to assert your control over her and what she does, lack of trust
- Thinking women are disposable, they are for your pleasure or use them for sex

Here's the thing, your mind is designed to protect you from pain not to make you happy or help you find the love of your life or to live a beautiful life.

At your core, your most primal self, you, we, all of us, are built to survive.

I acknowledge and honor you. You are right and did not deserve that. Please know this with my deepest compassion for what you have been through but until you get that wound in check, until you take responsibility for it and heal it, it will run your life. It will keep you playing small, protecting yourself, living in fear, guarding your heart and you will call it fate or destiny or just the way it is. That is no way to honor and live this beautiful life God gifted you with.

I'm calling you forward. You deserve better. You are here to feel good. Only you can say yes for you, only you can make that decision.

Embrace the unknown. The love of the good feminine woman you have always been worthy of is in the "unknown" on the other side of your fear. Allow yourself to feel the fear and do it anyway.

Cry Me a River

Do you know what I love about our society...? (Insert sarcasm) This might hurt a little.

People just love to complain and do absolutely *nothing* to change their lives. It's like you're either addicted to your own pain and suffering like maybe you actually enjoy it or maybe you like the attention you get when you play the victim and have your pity party again and again.

It's the blame game. And why not? That's easy, right? It takes the pressure off of you to actually do something about it because it's his fault or their fault or her fault.

We live in a society where it's popular to play the victim. God forbid, you take responsibility for your life and your choices. Let me give you a dose of tough love. *You* are the common denominator. No one else.

If you are an adult, and you are because no children are reading this book, then it is your responsibility to do better and to *be* better.

I am sure many of you are reading this and giving me the great big middle finger thinking you don't know what I have been through. And that's the thing, I do know, maybe not exactly, but I have been through some dark hard times with no one to count on or to help me besides me. Let me count the ways so you understand, the majority of my past was about pure survival, which included: neglect, abandonment, emotional abuse, almost being kidnapped twice, and almost drowning. I had 6 step dads by the age of 21, one stabbed my hand by accident and then told me I deserved it. A mom with not one nurturing bone in her body and parented my parent, two toxic husbands, one of which stalked me for a year, I had 4 PPOs against him and then told our then 3 small children of 3, 5, and 7 that your mommy is a whore (mind you, I was what you would call the "good girl") and she doesn't love you and there is more, but I'll stop here.

So, why am I telling you this? And why does it matter to you? Because I have come out on the other side of all that crap as a warrior of love, a better woman, a better human, more beautiful connections, an incredible career, attracting kings when I used to attract trolls, creating a more exquisite life than I ever thought possible. For no other reason I tell you this to stand for this truth: if I can do it, then so can *you*! You just need to learn how.

My life changed dramatically when I stopped the excuses. I did whatever it took to become better, to take control, responsibility, and accountability over my own life and what I wanted. To not allow what "happened to me" to keep me stuck in feeling sorry for myself, to understand myself more fully and why I did the things I did that kept me in the loop of suffering.

The real game changer was, that I became willing to do *whatever it took* to change the results from what I didn't want to what I did want.

Sometimes that has to be you first if you have no one else or you can't hire a professional to help. Sometimes it's a book like this that starts everything in the right direction for you, the inspiration from reading it to get the momentum moving. Once you make the decision and have the desire inside of you that you want things to be different, you want things to be better for you, and the ideas will start to come, listen, and follow wherever the direction leads you.

It's Not All Rainbows and Unicorns

Love. You know what's crazy? We all want love so badly but most of us suck at it if we're being honest with ourselves.

Most of us, when we love we love with conditions. We love when times are good and easy and run when things get hard. We love the good parts of the person, the good times. We love until someone better comes along. We love until the money runs out or as long as they are "hot." We love superficially and shallow.

Very few know how to love with depth and devotion, although we claim that's what we want. We are so afraid to be hurt that we only give part of our heart if we give any at all and we are quick to judge, criticize, and condemn when things aren't perfect.

Love, real love, true love, sacred love, devotional love, and pure love, has no room for that. When you have it, it will call you out and call you forward. It is the greatest gift and can transform your life into heaven on earth. You will feel exposed, raw, naked, and vulnerable and it will blow your heart wide open.

It will trigger you and expose all the wounds you thought you healed. It will expose all the ways you have forgotten the gift that you are all the ways you have believed you weren't good enough, lovable enough, or worthy enough and all the ways you believed you had to prove or please to get love. You cannot hide or stay small with real love.

If you are fortunate enough to share this rare love, it will probably scare you because you have never known this purest form of love. It is God's Divine selection for you. It will require you to be another version of yourself. The Self God made you to be.

Everyone says they want it, but the truth is not everyone is brave enough to allow themselves to receive it. Will you? Ask yourself if you are truly open to receiving this kind of love.

Relationship Houdini

*If you go around trying to "save" people, chances are you
wished someone would have saved you as a child.*

Some of our biggest fears in relationships are disconnection and
fear of abandonment, which stems from when we were babies and
young children.

So, when there is a conflict in the relationship that we don't agree
with or we want something else and are unaware of these patterns
(most people are until you start to see it within yourself), we'll just
leave. We will be the ones who does the abandoning, and not the ones
who get abandoned. *I'll leave you before you get the chance to leave
me.*

This is wounded relating and it often stems from our earlier
childhood life experiences.

Whereas when you are aware and consciously relating, you can
pause, self-reflect, and be introspective in your response, rather than
your knee-jerk automatic reaction of defending and protecting
yourself which has you operating from a place of fear and past hurtful
experiences instead of being present with what is.

When you have this awareness and are no longer running from
your past pain and can make different choices, even in the most heated
arguments, you then can remain calm in your heart and maintain the
connection, even if you need to walk away temporarily or leave the
room.

You can say things like, "I love you, babe, I just need some time
to process this and I'm here, I'm not going anywhere."

When you know yourself and what some of your own wounds are,
like the abandonment wound, you can communicate effectively to
your partner in that moment that this is triggering you and share how

that is making you feel. This allows your partner to reassure you that everything is going to be okay, and it actually helps you to heal that part of you. It shows you that you matter to them.

This then builds an even healthier, deeper connection and stronger bond, and have wonderful breakthroughs because it helps both of you to heal that abandonment wound and feel even safer within that relationship. Now you are creating an even deeper love, connection, and true intimacy with each other.

There are also times that it is a relationship that truly is not working for you anymore, and that's ok too, you realize it's not aligned with your greater good anymore and you are able to cut it off with grace and elegance, rather than ghosting, hiding or sabotaging it. It takes awareness of your own patterns, conditioning, and habits in relationships, then unlearning the old ways and relearning newer healthier ways of relating to actually create long-term permanent change and the amazing results that you truly want, which are hotter, happier, and healthier relationships.

Facing Yourself

Where you find your trauma, you find your treasure.

Everything we haven't processed or dealt with will show up in our lives including trauma in our adulthood until we deal with it.

How there is treasure in your trauma is when you deal with the trauma, and have the courage to dig into it and feel it and process it, and when applicable heal it, it becomes the very thing that propels you forward in life. You will become a stronger and better version of yourself. In my case, it helped me be of greater service not only to myself and my loved ones but also to the world. It becomes your greatest gift. That's why where you find your trauma you find your treasure. Look into where you hold shame, guilt, and fear around certain parts of you. Go within, and be introspective. Find out what's there for you underneath all the negative talk and "story." Get quiet, meditate, and go out into nature. It is in the stillness, in the quiet that we get the answers we seek. Listen for the whispers that point the way.

How You Feel About Yourself is Everything

The "Not Good Enough" Myth

If you feel that you are not good enough for *whatever*; you can fill in the blank. Maybe you tell yourself that you need to settle, you feel you are not good enough for a certain kind of partner, maybe you feel unworthy, unlovable, less than, maybe you feel or believe that you have to prove your value or worth.

However, it is that you feel to be true, that you believe consistently, will indeed create your "reality", basically what you see, hear, taste, touch, and smell and if it's a reality that you don't like you may even find yourself blaming it on "them," meaning anyone and everyone outside of yourself. But the truth is the power has always and will always be yours. Within your inner world, you create your outer world. Don't believe me? Look within your own experiences and you'll prove it to yourself. Examine your own thoughts, beliefs, expectations, and so-called truths. Reflect back to experiences where you were certain or expected something good or bad and it happened and you said, "I knew it!" Because you did it, you created it. You are more powerful than you realize.

Hot Mess

We all seem to want the "magic pill" in this life. The thing that is the correct answer, and we want it now; *instant gratification.*

There is something missing that most of you are not getting (that was me too in the past) and how could you, it was never taught to us. I'm not just talking about love, dating, and relationships, I'm talking about every aspect of your life. When I really understood it deep in my bones and embodied it, everything changed for the better.

If you want higher quality relationships, deeper connections, inner peace, fulfillment, love, joy, success, freedom, fun, authenticity, pleasure, play, confidence, humility, awe, and a love and appreciation for this precious gift of life and everyone in it., here's the magic pill: *your thoughts = your beliefs = how you feel = what you attract into your life.* Good or bad, positive or negative, right or wrong, whether you like it or not.

So, when you believe no good guys are out there, boom, there you go. There will be no good guys in your experience.

When you believe or expect no good women exist, boom, there you go, no good women.

And maybe you may be thinking, *yeah, but that's my reality, it's been my experience. There really aren't any good men or good women or at least not the kind I want…*

Or maybe you say or believe some of these common things I hear: "The dating pool has pee in it."

"There's no more real men."

"There's no attractive women my age."

"Relationships suck now, I'm giving up, women are mean and use me and I'm tired of it." Blah, blah, blah.

To that, I will tell you this. When you ask, it is always given, it is the divinity that is you, you are a creation of God, an aspect of God. You are a sacred and blessed being.

So, what are you asking for? Everything in life follows the path of least resistance, look at physics, look at nature. What is your dominant thought or belief? That is what you are asking for.

Those are the thoughts you will continue to think and therefore continue to believe because it is the law of physics, it is the path of least resistance. Sometimes when it seems to you that things don't go your way you will call it truth, reality, or fate, as in you are powerless. But in actuality, a belief is just a thought you keep thinking.

So, let's say you grew up in a household like mine, where your parents (in my case, step-parents), were critical and negative. Because that was your environment, negativity and criticism became your path of least resistance. Unless you actively change those deep-rooted thoughts, you'll keep defaulting to the same critical mindset, which ultimately attracts more negative experiences into your life.

If you don't like who or what kind of people or experiences are coming into your life, you have to change your thought process from what you don't want to what you do want.

It really is that simple, or it's hard, that's up to you. It's easy to do and it's easy not to do. It seems hard at first and then over time it becomes easier.

It doesn't happen overnight, after all, Rome wasn't built in a day.

It does take persistence, and your will, to unlearn and un-become all that they told you were, to become a different version of you. The one God (source, infinite intelligence), whatever you want to call the one I call God, made you to be.

The truth is, you have always been good, worthy, purposeful, valuable, free, powerful, and loved. Your life experiences or what "they" said may have just made you feel otherwise, but it's not true.

There is and has always been a power that flows to and through you, that power is God. The Creator of worlds. This is the truth that sets you free.

Shut-up and Wait

Ladies, listen up. I'm going to help you out here.

I was having a conversation with one of my male clients about the challenges with women, and he asked if I could record this. So here it is written. This is for you and on behalf of all the men out there.

Here's a challenge many of you ladies have and in full transparency, this was me too in the past. No one ever taught me this.

When you ask a man a question, please stop at the one question, pause, and give him time to answer. Do not shoot off 10 ten questions and look at him with the "what is taking you so long" look, and then make him bad or wrong for not answering you fast enough, or why he just gives up or shuts down and doesn't answer you.

Men are not like women, they are men, and we are different for a reason and I thank God for those differences. We are perfect complements to each other. So, he's not going to behave like one of your girlfriends. Many women say I want a real man and then when you have a real man you want him to be more like your girlfriends. He's not, he can't be because he's a man.

You don't *actually* want him to be, because then you wouldn't be attracted to him. It's polarity. It's chemistry, It's biology. Check-in with yourself and you'll see it's true. When your guy was more like "one of the girls" it turned you off.

So, ask the question and wait, *shut up and wait*. Yep, I said it, sometimes it needs to be said, sis.

Pause, do not speak, say nothing until he answers. Be there present with him. Understand that he wants to answer your question and he needs time to process it and articulate what it is he wants to say to best answer your question, and watch how much better he responds to you.

This is for all the men in your life, not just romantic partners.

Toxic Time Bombs

Interestingly, I have found that plenty of men don't even know that they are in toxic relationships. Crazy right? Why do you think that is?

Could it be that men have been so heavily conditioned to think it's their job to rescue women, to save women, that women are damsels in distress and weak, and so it's their duty to save them? Could it be that they had a mother who was cold and detached from her own heart and he had to try to win or prove his love, so he carried that into his adult relationships?

Could it be that they had a mother who was mistreated and had to do everything herself and so because the son loved his mother so much, he then thinks he has to prevent the women in his life from ever feeling that pain like his mother felt since he couldn't rescue her, he is subconsciously trying to rescue her through all his romantic partners?

I see this pattern a lot with the men who come to me for help. They almost never label their relationships "toxic." This fascinates me because the women I work with use that term all the time. Another thing I noticed is that men feel it is their duty to protect and provide for their partners (and kids) no matter what. If they don't, they believe they failed as a man. Even if she is detrimental, toxic, or downright poisonous they stick around. The truth is, that belief is an unresolved, unconscious response. It ultimately kills your polarity and when that happens, she stops desiring you.

Men, do yourself a favor and walk away in these cases. It is not your duty to fix or save anyone, you actually cannot anyway, that is your old programming, your past experiences running you. It is not the truth of who you are. You have not failed. God would never ask you to abandon yourself for someone else. You are just as important, you are just as valuable.

Your first duty, your first responsibility is to yourself, the divine being that you are, you are no good when you are coming from an empty place. When you are in service of others to your own detriment you are no good to anyone. This is not of service.

I know society has told you this is selfish, it is not. It is the essence of your power. Did God not make you too? I'm not telling you to end marriages or relationships, but I am telling you that you do not have the power to save anyone but yourself.

When you are in your Truth, your power, your connection to God, your authentic expression, your own magnificence, then you can help the world, then you can be of service to the greater good, then you can help others.

We'd Rather Binge Netflix Than
Face Ourselves

It seems that most people don't even know how to love, so we love selfishly and with conditions or barriers. I know that was me once upon a time. No one taught me, so how could I possibly have known. Maybe that's you too.

The modern dating world of love and relationships is loaded with past pains of past lovers, people bleeding their old wounds of the past all over each other, looking to fill this void of emptiness inside through going from partner to partner, relationship to relationship, porn, vapes, alcohol, work addiction, gambling, drugs, social media, television, *anything* to keep ourselves distracted from feeling the pain of loss, sadness, grief because it feels like it's too much. Sometimes it makes us feel like we're going to die. So instead of feeling those sensations, we become slaves to the distractions that keep us from feeling too much.

So instead of opening our hearts to let love in, we shield ourselves because the rejection of not being loved fully for who we are feels like it is too much for someone to hold. One of our caregivers, mothers or fathers, did not give us the love we deserved because they were unable to, they didn't know how because they never learned, so we feel this fear of not getting it again in our adult relationships. Yet the one thing we all long for and need is love. We are love. It is our core essence. We were birthed from love from God, our Creator. The entire world we live in is a creation of love.

To love is the greatest risk of all. We risk rejection, betrayal, and loss, yet if we have never loved truly, madly, or deeply, have we ever even lived? I say no. If we have not allowed our hearts to be obliterated open to feel the depth of true love, the deepest, most intimate profound connection of soulmate love, what are we even doing here? How are you loving yourself? Do you even like yourself? Or do you constantly allow the mind chatter to tell you all the ways you are unlovable, not good enough, and undeserving, so you cut yourself off from love.

Allow yourself to go into the body and feel any sensations that arise. Feel. Feel it all! Feel the anger, the betrayal, the rage, the grief, whatever your situation is or was, and *let it out*. Express it through tears, laughter, screaming, beating the crap out of something (note I did not say someone) or yell it out, do whatever it takes, but please don't hold it in anymore. Let it out, express it, and stop holding it in and taking it out on yourself. It's poison and it is slowly destroying you from the inside. You can do any of these in the safety of your own house or go out in the middle of nowhere and do this.

Here's the thing that many don't realize, there is nothing more triggering or healing than a romantic relationship if you let it. You can do all the "personal development" work you want alone and I highly encourage it because we all have our own inner work to do, but there is a place in union, in romantic love that will feel uncomfortable because nothing pulls out your core wounds that need healing like romantic love.

True love, soulmate love, can feel like a death has occurred at first because your heart is being ripped wide open, with nowhere to hide anymore because that's exactly what it is, the death of the old self and the merging into another into true love. Many of us have never experienced or seen a healthy love modeled. If that's you, please start by loving yourself, especially the parts that the world has told you are bad or wrong, start with those, those are your core wounds and your biggest opportunity for transformation.

Ask yourself how can you allow yourself to be cracked wide open to love today? How can you love more truly, madly, and deeply?

Rescue Ranger

If you grew up in an environment as a child where it was your job to take care of everyone else and nurture everyone else, where your needs came last behind everyone else, then you may find that you struggle to try to "fix" things in your relationships. You may make it your job to try to save them from feeling the pain, but the reality is, you cannot do this for anyone and it is not your job either. And this may make you come off as too much, either too needy or too controlling, which will end up pushing the person you want away because they need the space to figure this out themselves. Your heart is in the right place, but it's your childhood wounds that are running the show.

For women, this can be a thing we have been raised to do especially if we had to parent our parent or "grow up fast" and take on adult responsibilities like caring for our younger siblings or having a parent who was emotionally immature and unknowingly or knowingly used you as their therapist.

This can have damaging repercussions on your adult romantic relationships. Healing your inner child is part of the journey to becoming whole again, to being your true self. Any time you feel this part of you come up, be with it, full presence, your acceptance, full unconditional love, and tell yourself "I got you, you are safe now, you are loved, you matter." And anything else that just organically comes up for you. Feel the discomfort within your body, validate it, validate that part of you, that little boy or little girl, acknowledge how it feels, any sensations or thoughts that come up, and give it all your pure presence and unconditional love. Ask within: What do you need? What do you want? Why are you here? Journal what comes up.

The Inner Glow

Many people are obsessed with outside transformation and I understand that. It feels good to look good.

To have a healthier body but many, I'd say actually most, don't realize that there is more to this transformation. It's the inner part.

While the inner and outer both matter, I'd say the inner is most crucial because that is what actually shapes your "outer" reality.

With such an emphasis on how we look to everyone else, let's remember that you are a mind, a body, and a soul. Each one is as important as the other. So just as it is important to take care of your beautiful temple, you only get one, it is equally important to take care of yourself spiritually, mentally, emotionally, your heart, and all of you.

You can be the hottest person in the room and if you neglect the rest of you that I just spoke of you will often find yourself feeling like something is missing, maybe feeling empty, unfulfilled, looking outside of yourself searching for someone else to make you happy or fulfilled when all you really need to do is go within and start to give yourself that same type of love.

Drag Your Ass out of that Rut

For me, there's no reason to stay stuck, complacent, or unhappy. And it sometimes comes off as harsh. But, really the truth is we have all suffered in some way, we all have wounds, we all have bad things that have happened. I haven't met one person yet who hasn't had a story. And I have so much compassion for that. Often there's a process, a grieving, a sadness, sometimes a darkness (darkness is not evil) we need to go into to get to the other side. But don't stay there, don't stay in that dark depressive space for too long, it's detrimental to your well-being. Sometimes you have to drag yourself out of your pain, and your anger to finally start to feel better.

Some great ways to feel better now, today, tomorrow, and any day and every day is even better.

- Get outside into nature
- Get out into the sun, feel the earth underneath your bare skin
- Even take a nature bath, lay on the earth, the trees, the rocks, the beach, the earth is alive and has a magnetic pulse
- Disconnect from all your electronic devices or at least choose consciously when you are going to engage, don't just mindlessly scroll. It can cause you to feel overwhelmed, stressed, and anxious, know when to detach and unplug
- Eat real food, meaning if God made it, it's real, keep the fake food out of your system as much as you can
- Work out and move your body, we were not built to be sedentary
- Be nice, be kind to people, (especially yourself), open a door, maybe smile at a stranger, if you see something you like about someone say so, or donate your time
- Consume healthy things; meaning, people, television, music, and books, what you allow your mind, body, and soul to consume needs to be healthy… *because you become it*
- Don't forget to play, your inner child loves to have fun and you are never too old

- Meditate. If you don't know how look up "guided meditations" and choose the one you like
- Pet your pet, or someone else's if you don't have one. It releases serotonin and dopamine, your natural "feel good" chemicals in your brain. In fact, almost all of these things I listed make you "feel good" naturally

Cash Doesn't Make The King

Dear Men:

Making money doesn't make you the man. When did we decide this? When did we put all the power and pressure on men thinking they were the only ones? Women can make as much money and it doesn't have to take away your manhood unless you believe it does.

Why does all the pressure have to rest on a man's shoulders? Who decided this? And why have we bought into it?

If you really give it some thought, does it make sense to you that one gender is entitled to and also burdened with generating all the wealth?

Provide and protect? What if part of the providing is providing love, friendship, pleasure, joy, safety, connection, fun, play, loyalty, someone who feels like and is a true partner, side by side walking this life together, your best friend that you can't keep your hands off of.

Who decided women can't be wealthy and that the only way we can have wealth is through men or through manipulation?

Women, you don't need a man to have the lifestyle that you want. You can create it yourself – the money, the houses, the clothes, the vacations, along with the freedom to choose whatever you want.

You have the same God-given ability to create that too. You, we, and men have just bought into a very big, long, lie. We have been conditioned, even brainwashed into believing that we cannot also be wealthy.

What if we took all that pressure away from all of us?

What if you are the woman in your family who finally breaks the generational belief that women can't make money, that women are the lesser sex, and that women need a man for this and that? Could this be why they find themselves in bad relationships attracting the "wrong" men?

What if it's all been a lie that we have all bought into for *too* long? And this has nothing to do with the boss babe hyper-independent "I don't need a man" movement, which is based on fear and lack, and nothing is empowering about it.

This is about questioning what society has told you, questioning your own beliefs and what lies you may have bought into. Even question me and this book. Question everything.

We all want to be loved and appreciated for *who* we are *not* how someone can benefit from having us in their lives.

Question everything that you have believed as truth and you will unravel many of the things that keep you miserable, fearful, disempowered, trapped, stuck, etc.

This is the path to freedom, to your truth, and not the truth you have been sold.

God isn't a Sky Cop

There is not some God in the sky condemning you and some people and then loving others. There is only love.

If you are in an unhealthy or bad relationship with people who don't treat you like the incredibly valuable person you are it's more than likely because you have an unhealthy, bad relationship with yourself.

Maybe you don't feel worthy of a good man or good woman because you have never experienced it and maybe mom or dad made you feel like nothing you ever did was good enough. So you find yourself going around trying to prove your worth and your value in your relationships.

Or maybe you are expecting them to treat you badly, cheat on you, or do something similar to what your past lover did to you that you didn't like. Maybe you don't feel like you are good enough so you put on masks and pretend to be someone you think "they" might like. You wear a guard around your heart, act aloof, and pretend you're being mysterious and sexy.

So what is my point you may ask?

Look, you're not being punished, you're not broken, and you're not less than. You're just in a cycle that's only going to change when you change the way you see yourself. There's no "sky cop" God keeping you from the love you deserve. It's all you.

Here's the truth: when you value yourself, it's like a vibration that radiates out, pulling in people who value you, too. When you stop looking for others to fill your worth and start showing up as the real, raw, unguarded you, the right people are drawn to that. The wrong ones? They fall away.

So, drop the masks, let go of what didn't serve you in the past, and show up as you — the you who's ready to be loved for exactly who you are. You are good enough, you are worth it, and love — the real, soul-deep kind — is within your reach.

It's Time to Get Your Balls Back

Dear Men:

It was never your job to save her. It was never your job to take her disrespect. If you desire a feminine woman you are going to have to stop believing "them." You will have to stop being the "nice guy." You will have to stop being the pushover. You will have to stop worrying about what "they" think.

And you will have to stop letting her control you and "wear the pants." You will have to stop letting her criticize you and have boundaries and you'll have to start being the true man God made you to be. If you want a more feminine woman, *be* a more masculine man.

A woman doesn't want to wear the pants, tell you what to do, and lead in the relationship… but she will if has to. Don't point the finger at her and tell her all the ways she needs to stop being so bossy. Don't point your finger at her telling her all the ways she needs to stop being so controlling. When did you become so passive? Point your finger at yourself and become the man who leads by example. Point your finger at yourself and ask, when did you forget who the fuck you were?

When did you stop respecting and loving yourself? When did you forget your power?

Do you want her to be softer, surrendered, and in her authentic feminine nature? Be the man she feels safe enough to do that with. And this does not take away her responsibility to become receptive to your masculinity.

You cannot rescue or save her enough to ever make that happen. That is her work and her work alone.

In a world that makes it easy to blame others, be the one who looks in the mirror and takes responsibility for how you got to where you are in the first place, and then be courageous enough to be the man

God made you to be. And I promise you will become irresistible to the *true* feminine woman.

There is Nothing Wrong with You, But…

I want to tell you something, no matter what you are going through in your life, there is absolutely nothing wrong with you.

You are not broken and you do not need to be fixed or saved.

But if you are suffering in your relationships, or suffering at all in any aspect of your life,

If you find yourself in more moments of pain than pleasure in any of your relationships or life,

If you find yourself in more moments of fear than faith in any of your relationships,

Then even though there is nothing inherently wrong with *you*, something definitely is wrong.

And it is often our unmet childhood needs that play out in our adult relationships until we deal with them.

When we are children, our experiences with those around us, especially our primary caregivers shape how we feel about others and especially how we feel about ourselves. And you don't have to have a terrible childhood for these experiences to still continue to impact you in your adult life.

Many people grow up thinking I just had a normal childhood, which is often true.

But unless your parents were the rare ones who were emotionally self-resourced, chances are you experienced situations that are still running your life undetected.

These experiences leave imprints and marks within your body, your nervous system your unconscious subconscious (not literally, of course) and will run you unknowingly in your adult relationships. It's like your body is frozen within the time or times of that events or events or experiences.

I also want to let you know that contrary to what we have been taught by "normal" society standards, you are not here to suffer. There is no gold medal you earn for the amount you can take or endure or suffer through.

Start allowing the awareness of seeing the suffering in your relationships and all aspects of your life that something requires your attention, your examination, and your introspection.

In my experience through all my years of guiding, teaching, and coaching people, the one thing I see again and again is the relationships we have with ourselves are the ones that need the care, the love, and the attention the most.

It is often the relationship we have with ourselves that gets the most neglect and the least amount of care. But when you transform the relationship to self, and not "self-centered" from a place of ego, more so a place of being centered within Self, the place and source of your Divinity, things just start to seem to work out for you, for your greater good. You are and always have been a blessed being.

Is Your Inner Jerk Killing Your Joy?

I don't care how well you take care of your looks, or your outside appearance, if your inner talk is full of disrespect, self-loathing, criticism, judgment, and contempt… you will make yourself feel terrible. You will feel stressed, and have anxiety, panic attacks, sadness, grief, and depression. Unfortunately, given enough time you will make yourself sick or diseased.

You are a mind, a body, and a soul simultaneously… treat yourself accordingly. Pay attention to what you allow yourself to consume, not just in the foods you eat, but in the content you watch, what you listen to, and who you take advice from. Be conscious consumers of everything that you allow within your mind, body, and soul, everything that you see, hear, taste, touch, and smell to take in and believe. Question everything, and tune into your intuition to lead you, it's God talking to you.

And here's the thing: you always have a choice. So don't you think it's about time to choose something better for you, like right here and right now?

You can keep letting that inner critic run wild, dragging down every joy you could feel and every dream you could dare to reach for. Or, you can take charge of this inner world of yours, and become your own fierce protector and compassionate guide. When you love yourself enough to guard what enters your mind, nourish your body, and uplift your spirit, you become the true architect of your life.

Joy, peace, and love are not just things that happen to you — they're states of being you create, moment by moment, by how you choose to treat yourself. You are worthy of the highest love and the most vibrant life, and it starts with you.

Time to Be a Bad Bitch

Dear Women:

Being a good girl is killing us. Women have been conditioned for thousands of years to be the good girl. The good wife, the good daughter, the good mother, the good giver, the pleaser. We have been taught the belief that we need to be pleasing to others. And it is making us sick, poor, miserable, depressed, burned out, and bitter.

Did you know that in the 18th and 19th centuries, women were labeled or diagnosed for being "hysterical," and that was common for women because they considered women more lazy and irritable? We have been demonized and told we are bad or wrong or evil if we don't comply. From an early age, little girls are taught to please, to be nice, not to speak up, and not to be too much.

And in that space to comply we betray ourselves, our own wants, needs, and desires to make everyone else around us pleased with us.

We have sex with our husbands when we really don't want to because that's what a good wife does. We run ragged taking care of everyone else; husbands, children, friends, colleagues, and neglect ourselves because that's what a good woman does.

We give and we give and we give until there's nothing left of us because that's what a good woman does, she's a giver, but not a receiver, that would be "bad."

And this shame and guilt we carry for *not* being good leave its path of destruction in how we are feeling in our bodies; fatigue, diseases, sickness, burnout, exhaustion, numbness, and inability to feel pleasure, all take their toll on our bodies. It is because we have been taught, brainwashed, and conditioned to be this way over time, over and over again, within ourselves, our mothers, and our ancestry and we look around and see most women on this hamster wheel, and we ignore our own inner voice. Our intuition, our wisdom, screaming at us to stop and get off the hamster wheel is what society has brainwashed us of who we are. You are not here to comply, you are not here to be the good girl and to obey and to please and appease.

Enough of us being labeled and labeling each other as bitches, crazy, cold, and evil, enough of the slut shaming and catty judging. Things like, "Oh, she must have slept with someone to be where she's at." This has to stop.

The truly feminine woman in her pure essence is not the pleasing "good girl." She is confident, bold, comfortable in her own skin, sexy, loving, sensual, kind, joyful, intuitive, wise, cunning, open, in flow with life, wild, fierce, audacious, and free, she is in my words, a bad bitch (where "bad" in this case is the epitome of the best).

In pleasing everyone else, you are betraying yourself, and you, your mind, your body, your soul, and your life are paying the price. You are not here to please others, contrary to what society has told you.

You are here to please yourself. This is your life and only you know what's best for you, because only you live in your body, feel what you feel, and experience what you experience. You are here to have fun, be joyful, feel peace, love, play, and the freedom to be the Divine being that you came here to be.

Do the things that bring you more of that, and stay only in relationships with other people that feel more like those things, that feel good in your soul, in your heart.

The Moment I Realized I Was the Problem

The most important question I ever asked myself was *What is wrong with you that you keep attracting and choosing these toxic men? Two divorces Melanie, WHAT is wrong with you?*

That was my dialogue with myself about 7 years ago. It was a pivotal moment in my life that would change *everything* as I knew it. You see, the majority of my life I was literally in survival mode, and I unknowingly kept myself there by the unconscious negative beliefs I took on about myself without even realizing from the people in my environment.

The day that I asked myself that question I had no idea of the how, the what, the who on what was going to come next, I just knew that there was no way I was going to get into one more toxic relationship… EVER. And not coming from a guarded heart, more so coming from a place of I am going to figure this pattern out and change it for good, so I can have the kind of beautiful, loving, healthy relationship I wanted. The game changer for me? I realized I was the common denominator. Yes, they had plenty of toxic traits, but who chose them? Me. I chose these men, these were not arranged marriages. I chose them of my own free will.

So, my question to myself was why would you get into relationships like that in the first place? What part of you is okay with being treated poorly? What part of you feels like she needs to prove her value? What part of you feels like it is your job to sacrifice your own happiness to make someone else happy? What part of you believes you need to give and give and give and get little reciprocation in return? And why?

So, I examined my inner world, I did the inner work, I did more work on me than anyone I know, and I spent six figures with what I would have called back then "fixing me." But I was never broken, to begin with, I never needed to be fixed, there was nothing inherently wrong with me. The same is true for you. But something was definitely wrong and that's what I set out to excavate and understand and do whatever it took to change it.

What happened next would be the most ineffable thing! Genuine inner peace, when I always felt like my stomach was in knots, deep self-love when before I had the worst inner critic you ever heard, attracting kings when I used to attract trolls, so much joy and love for life, play, fun, beautiful connections with so many wonderful people, opportunities, experiences, and the knowing that I was destined to teach this to others too.

I live a completely different life now, virtually unrecognizable from my past. And I don't tell you all of this to brag, I tell you because if I can do it, so can you!

Your inner world, meaning how you talk to yourself, how you really feel about yourself, the love or lack thereof of yourself, your inner dialogue, the thoughts, the feelings, and the beliefs about you and the world around you will reflect itself to you in your outer world. There is no magic pill out there to save you or a person, it's you.

Do you want better relationships, deeper quality connections, genuine joy, fun, play, and peace, to be in love with life? Then you have to do the inner work to remove all the lies you have taken on and told yourself over the years. Examine yourself, introspect.

You are powerful, you are valuable, you are worthy, you always have been and always will be, and you have never had to prove it to anyone else other than yourself. You are a Divine being, an aspect of God in human form.

Our relationships with others, "good or bad", will always be a reflection of the relationship we have with ourselves, a mirror if you will.

You, we, none of us are not here to suffer, contrary to what most people think and believe, you are here to enjoy this life, to feel good, to have fun, expand, to become more, to be, do, and have what you desire.

If that is not your present reality, then I invite you to look within and see how you might be getting in your own way.

Why Staying for the Kids is Sometimes More Harmful

I'd rather die than do what my mom did to me to my kids.

I remember thinking that. Bouncing from my mom's boyfriends, stepdads, and multiple relationships all the while feeling like what I thought didn't matter, feeling like collateral damage. And so when I became a mom, I swore like hell that I would not be the kind of mom she was and I would never get a divorce because in my mind because of the pain I felt as a child, I never wanted my children to endure even an ounce of that. But what I soon came to realize within my own experience is that believing that "Staying for the kids" has become a belief, a conditioned way of being that if you leave you are somehow the "bad one." So it brings up so much judgment around what you perceive about yourself. And then we often will stay in unhealthy relationships to appease others, to not be judged or criticized.

I am not saying anyone should get divorced and I am not saying anyone should stay together for the kids. Only you truly know what's best within your given experience. But is staying together really in the children's best interest all the time? I say no.

I had to examine that thought within myself during the compilation of divorcing my children's father. You see, I was 100% against getting divorced. In my mind, divorce meant I was becoming my mom. I knew how painful it felt because I endured the pain as a child having 6 stepdads. I would have rather died than give that same experience and pain to my children.

So, there I stayed in a loveless, toxic marriage with obligatory sex that made me want to vomit, but I did it anyway because I felt it was my "duty" as a wife. Can I just tell you how gross that felt, it was self-betrayal and it made me hate myself.

Then add all the toxicity: the silent treatment, the intentional isolation from family and friends, the control, the belittling, the brainwashing of how superior he was to me, that I could not be, do, or have anything without him, that became my life as his goal was to break my spirit slowly chipping away at me little by little to go "unnoticed." And here I was staying for the kids???!!

The truth is, they gave me the courage to leave actually. They inspired it, It was actually for them that I left.

These insights kept coming to me. *If I stay, I am showing my daughter how a man should treat her.* Hell no. *If I stay, I am showing my sons how they should treat a woman.* No way. *This ends with me. I am ending this toxic pattern in my life, and in my children's lives. My children will not carry this generational pattern on. This ends now.*

And I never looked back! I felt free for the first time in a really long time. So for you, if you find yourself here, contemplating a divorce, is it good for the kids, is it bad for the kids, what will "they" think of me, don't make any decision about this based on fear. Choose based on peace, from a calm state of being, look within, and introspect. It does not make you selfish to walk away, sometimes actually the most selfish or easiest thing to do is to stay and the hardest is to walk away, it takes tremendous courage and it is not easy.

I am not here to push you in either direction. I am only here to spark your own inner knowing and truth. If there is a chance to repair your relationship and rekindle the love, that might be worth exploring. But if it's toxic, distant, or lacking genuine affection, is that really the marriage you want? Is that the model you want your children to follow? Remember, kids reflect who we *are* more than what we *say*. It is up to you to decide which example you want to set.

Shoulda, Woulda, Coulda

People often say they want one thing, but then settle for another that is nowhere near what they said they want. Why do we do these things?

It usually derives from some deep-buried feelings like I don't deserve what I want, so I might as well just settle for what's right in front of me or I'm not good enough, I'm not worthy, etc. Or they get trapped, guilted, or shamed into what society has said they should do.

For example, a man gets a woman pregnant and marries her because of the belief that's what a "good" man does because he "should" it's the "right" thing to do. Meanwhile, he may have just created himself a life sentence into misery shackled to what "they" say he "should" do.

Look around you… how many people do you actually know who are truly really happy, living their best life? There are not a lot. So what do we continue to listen to "them" — them meaning anyone besides ourselves, anyone besides our own inner wisdom, our own intuition, our own connection to God within us? Usually, it is because we are conditioned that way. It's a thought pattern thought enough that it becomes a belief.

Society loves to put us in judgment boxes like "this makes you right and this makes you wrong, this makes you good and this makes you bad." And then we do that too. And then we judge others and we judge ourselves based on these so-called "boxes."

Why? Because it makes us feel safer to have the perception of controlling situations to "control" others. The truth is, the only thing within our control is ourselves.

Your spirit, your soul, the part of you who never dies, does not live within that space. Everything is done unto you as you command, nothing is ever done to you.

So why do we say, for example, "I want this and that" in our relationships, but then when that very kind of relationship is right in front of us, we have no idea what to do with it? Because of these things that I have been speaking about in this book.

So here's the truth, plain and simple: those "shoulds" and "coulds" are nothing but illusions. They're chains that keep you from your own path, from discovering the kind of love, freedom, and joy that's waiting for you on the other side. Life isn't about living in the safety of someone else's rules — it's about daring to live in alignment with your own.

When you listen to yourself, really tune in past the noise, you begin to realize that all the answers you need are within you. The part of you that is connected to something greater, the part of you that knows what it's here to do, is wise beyond any societal "should" or inherited guilt. It's time to break free from the trap of living by someone else's story and start creating your own.

You don't have to settle for the life society expects. You can choose the life your soul craves. You can stand up, unlearn, and rewire, becoming the kind of person who lives with the fullness of joy, true to yourself, with a purpose that's your own. So here's your permission slip: let go of the "shoulds," honor the whispers of your own spirit, and finally step into the life that's been waiting for you all along.

Because that's what real freedom looks like, and it's yours for the taking.

Fear Factor

*Why do we sometimes ruin a good thing with a seemingly great
partner or relationship?*

We sabotage it. Why? Because self-sabotage is actually self-
protection. Somewhere deep down in our unconscious, we believe that
person will leave us, hurt us, and abandon us, so what do we do
instead? We hurt them or leave them or abandon them. Self-survival
(protection) at its most primal self

But what if we stayed? What if we felt all the uncomfortable
feelings and still stayed and communicated that to him or her instead
of doing our usual hiding? Imagine how good that could feel — to
truly allow yourself to be seen fully and still loved and accepted.

What if that person turned out to be the one you have always
wanted? *The one you prayed for.* What if? You'll never know unless
you take the risk, step into the uncomfortableness, and allow it.

The Great Unbecoming

When you feel like you are being squeezed and your world feels like it's falling apart, maybe your relationships are falling apart, you lose your job or you lose your money, or you're getting another divorce. You feel like you are in the "darkness" (depression, anger, rage, fear, grief, etc.). I want you to know this: You are entering a portal, a transformation, the ability to choose differently instead of the same old way.

You are *unbecoming* all that you are not to *become* all that you are.

The old patterns, limiting beliefs, societal conditioning, and childhood traumas, i.e. "old you," cannot come into this portal. The old you will not get you there.

So, you are not being punished, you are not bad or wrong and you are not failing, you are not broken when these things are happening though I know it can definitely *feel* that way.

You are becoming the *real* you that you set out to be in this lifetime. The old version of you must "die" (not literally) for a new version to be reborn. Some have referred to this as the dark night of the soul.

What's happening to you is a good thing! It is an incredible thing! Allow it, let go trust and surrender to it. Be with all aspects of you that come up, the so-called good and bad. Just as a diamond has to undergo immense pressure to become itself to become beautiful, so do you sometimes.

We rarely can transform into our greatness when we are "comfortable" or complacent. You are not just a human, you are divinity, you are an extension of God, of Source, of the Creator of all things seen and unseen. That power that creates worlds is within you.

You are not here by accident, nothing is. You have come here to experience this beautiful humanity and the variety, the contrast, How else are you supposed to know what you desire unless you experience some things you don't want and vice versa?

You are not here to suffer, suffering is an effect from being out of alignment with God, from your own knowing of your own power.

You may have just forgotten. So I'm here to remind you who you really are. You are the most powerful force in this world. God is flowing to and through you always… act accordingly.

Not Always "The Good Girls"

Dear Men:

The majority of the world's perception of women is screwed up. We are not all love and light, there is plenty of darkness and I don't mean false perceptions of evil or bad.

We do not need to be saved or rescued. We are not a project to be fixed. We are not damsels in distress waiting for the white knight. We are not evil and we are not the reason Adam ate the apple. We are here to be your partner and to walk side by side with you. We are not the weaker sex, our strength does not come from our muscles.

We see and feel things you don't, it is one of our superpowers. We cannot do all the same things men can do, nor do we want to. We are not sluts or whores nor are we here to use sex as a weapon or to manipulate you. We are not here to fit into your mold.

We do not run on this world's 24/7 clock, we have an internal clock that is in harmony with the different cycles of the moon and the earth, time is a "man-made" construct, it is not real and not made by God.

We are not here for you to have power over us or to tell us who we can be or what we can do. We are not here to mother grown men. We feel deeply even if we don't say a word. We are not here to fit into any box.

We are not the good girls. We were literally burned at the stake because weak people did not understand the gift of our power, and most women have forgotten too. We are not here to please you.

We are the co-creators of life within our wombs. We are a force of nature.

We are the witches, the healers, the oracles, the seers, and the wise women. We are the ones who initiate men into becoming kings.

Look around in history *any* man who became great, didn't do so until he met his beloved, his queen.

Women: It's time to remember who you truly are as a Divine feminine being.

Men: The right woman is a gift and will help rise into the man you came here to be, the wrong woman... well, she can destroy you if you let her.

Choose wisely.

Know-It-Alls

In this information age, we have all become a bunch of know-it-alls but most still don't know shit.

We can literally google just about anything, and get a multitude of answers, and information right in the palm of our hands, and yet we are still overweight, unhealthy, unfulfilled, depressed, sick, broke, lonely, divorced, diseased, and stressed.

Why? Because knowledge really is not power, the knowing within your thinking mind is not enough. You can listen to all the TED talks or podcasts, YouTube videos, reels, TikTok, etc., but you are missing the biggest key that most won't tell you or don't even know and that is the embodiment of that knowledge.

Until this so-called "I know," I know everything but I'm still miserable, I am still lying to myself about who I really am.

Until you get this knowledge within your body, within your being, within your nervous system, your consciousness, until you feel it as truth within every cell, until there is zero doubt that you do not actually know, you won't actually have the results, the changes, the experiences, the money, the relationships, the body, etc.

If knowing was the answer, especially with all the ways we can find information we would all have everything we have ever wanted. Think about it.

If simply knowing something was enough, we all would be rich, we all would be healthy and hot, we all would be in careers we love, we all would be in beautiful relationships with the loves of our lives, and we all would be fulfilled and living our best life. But most people don't even have a fraction of that list. This is one of the main reasons why. This is why when I read books I read them over and over and over, which I encourage you to do with this book too. It does not sink in deep enough with one reading for this or any other book. Repetition and consistency are key. Plus, doing the work to heal the parts that are preventing you from having the things you desire.

Said another way: Until you take this knowledge and turn it into something that lives in you — something that shifts how you breathe, how you move, how you respond, and how you show up in the world — you're just collecting ideas. Real wisdom doesn't come from hearing about it once or reading a book once. It's built through repetition, through living it over and over until it becomes part of you until it reshapes you from the inside out.

So don't just skim the surface here. Let this be more than a feel-good read that sits on your shelf while your life stays the same. Take this book, this work, these truths, and dig deep. Read it again. Do the work. Make it real in your body, in your heart, and in the way you live each day. This is how you get to that life you crave — alive, on fire, and truly embodied.

What if "Good Enough" Was Always the Truth?

What if you knew you were good right now? What if you knew you were worthy now? That you deserved everything you have ever wanted and maybe you just asked the wrong people unknowingly.

What if the things that make you feel bad about yourself are the things that need most of your love and understanding? What if you could allow yourself to feel all the hard feelings that made you feel bad and love them exactly as you are now?

It is often the things that feel the hardest to allow ourselves to feel that are the very things that liberate us and set us free. We think feeling bad is actually bad, but it's really not.

It's easy to feel the good things or to want to chase the dopamine hits and sometimes for some of us it's actually easier to just stay stuck in our anger, fear, worry, and doubt because we know it so well. We have become best friends. But, I want you to know that no part of beating yourself up will ever make you feel better. No part of telling yourself all the ways you suck, no part of your inner critic that whips you into submission will ever lead to a beautiful life. So, what if choosing to feel good no matter what, was the answer to a beautiful life?

Not when you heal, not when your life turns around, not when you have the perfect partner, not when things get better... but right now.

Feeling good, loving and accepting yourself right now exactly as you are, choosing to feel better now, choosing to look for all the good that is here right now and focus on that, and reminding yourself that everything always works out for you no matter what.

I promise you, you were not put here to suffer. You were put here to experience joy and love and fun and fulfillment and freedom, I know you have suffered, as have I, and there has been tremendous growth in it, not as a form of punishment, but more of an opportunity to go within and examine yourself and all the ways you tell yourself you are unlovable, undeserving, unworthy and then to love those parts, accept and acknowledge, validate. Of course, you feel this way. Whatever thing you are going through makes you feel this way and at the same time, this is a gift that brings you within to love yourself anyway, even deeper, unconditionally the way that you always deserved to be loved. Maybe you never received it from anyone else before. So now, you have to unlearn all those messages that convinced you that you were not worthy of love.

There isn't a part of you that needs to prove that any part of you is deserving or worthy or good enough to anyone other than yourself. Start to speak to yourself with more praise, more compliments, and start to celebrate yourself more; the little wins.

Look for more ways to show yourself how amazing you are instead of how you can improve, maybe even start to write love notes to yourself every day: "Dear me, I am awesome. I am good. I am Divine. I am an aspect of God. I have a big, beautiful heart. I love you, etc." Just start to let those things flow and look for the easy things that come to you naturally.

If you are having trouble, start with what you needed to hear when you were little What do you wish someone had told you? How do you wish you were spoken to as a child?

Remember, you will date the same person in a different body until you do the work to heal the parts of you who chose that person to begin with.

Boss Babes and Doormat Dudes

There has been a downfall in marriage and healthy relationships. Fewer people are getting married. Many people today just don't want to do this marriage thing anymore.

Even though statistically divorce rates are down, it's only because not as many people are getting married. And there are a lot of contributors to it that some of you may or may not like.

One of the factors is that women are making it way too easy for guys to be in "situationships," and so there's a lack of courting, there's a lack of intimacy, there's a lack of chivalry, romance, and dating. Why? Because they'll give it to you on the first date you don't even have to work for it.

And you know what? This may trigger some of you, but it's too bad. I'm here to have some *real* talk!

So that's one contributor that I've seen and of course, my perspective is unique from most because of who I am and what I do.

Another thing is that society is turning more women into men and men into women and I mean energetically. What I mean by this is, that men are way more passive, they have become way more like doormats. They are getting into relationships with women where they "allow" them and I use that word lightly, to be controlled and criticized by women, instead of standing up for themselves and having boundaries. Simply put they are being emasculated. This is often related to wounds men have around the mother or the feminine in general that are still unaddressed.

And then if you go on the women's side of it, there's the whole boss babe movement, which is complete BS as far as I'm concerned with the way society is creating it. She's a hyper-independent woman living in masculine energy and she's like, "I got this. I don't need you. I don't need a man because I make the money now and I can do this all by myself!" It often comes down to the unaddressed wounds around her father or the masculine in general, that haven't been resolved. Actually, secretly all she wants is a "real man." A good man, but she can never have a real man (until she addresses these wounds) because *she is the man*, so she's a repellent to the very kind of man she wants.

Unfortunately, instead of us coming together the way that we were created to be, we're in competition and conflict with each other and then many men are basically thinking, "Forget it! I'm just done! I've been with so many women and they ripped my heart out!" They feel this has just ruined them, so they are walking away and staying single.

With the women, it's the same thing, "I've been mistreated! I got married and I bought into the fairytale and I gave up my career and then he left me and left me with nothing. Now I'm working all these jobs to take care of these kids!" Subsequently, they are also staying single.

Many are declaring, "My kids are everything and I am just going to concentrate on them." Children are important, but this is usually a decision out of fear, guarding their heart, they simply do not trust that they will not get into another relationship with the "wrong one" again, so they don't. This increases people being more bitter, jaded, resentful, and just plain over it.

Another contributing factor is, that men are more feminine than they have ever been and women are way more masculine than they have ever been. Which is keeping us divided more and more and more. So why would we want to come together?

And then add, that sex has become really easy, really, really, really, easy... for both sides to obtain than it used to be, again, I'm not disregarding anyone's personal choices, everybody should do whatever it is that they think is right for them. Zero judgment here. I am just pointing out things that I see as a huge shift.

It used to be a man would have to properly date a woman; court her, romance her, love her, protect her, and provide for her (and not necessarily financially). With the increase of dating apps, "the grass is greener" mentality, and people still dating from an unconscious wounded space within, it's no wonder people are so unhappy in modern-day relationships.

There are also currently the men out there who want to court, date, and romance and be in a beautiful relationship, but even they are concerned and scared of all this, "I don't need a man." crap, so they don't. They are tired of trying to be the masculine man that they are and hearing things like, "Don't get the door for me! How dare you! How dare you do that! I can get my own door! What do you think? I am weak!"

There is so much more to unpack here. So what do you do about it you may ask? You may have noticed a common thread in this book. We need to go within ourselves. Examine the unhealed wounds we still may be operating from the unconscious. Maybe even take some time away from dating for a bit to clear your head. Give yourself some space to sit with it, read some books like this on the subject, hire a coach, hire a therapist, take an online course, go to a retreat, meditate; be alone in the quiet, and follow your inner wisdom. This will lead you to your next step.

WTF is Wrong with Me?!

Sometimes, the old you must die for a newer, better version of yourself to be reborn.

I don't mean literally that your body must die. I mean mentally, spiritually, and emotionally. This is truly the definition of a Phoenix who rises from the ashes. This is what happened to me 7 years ago (actually *for* me).

I came to the realization during my second divorce truly wondering wtf was wrong with me. Every ounce of me felt broken. How am I here at this point in my life? How did I get here? This is *not* how I pictured my life to be.

Have you been there? Maybe you are there now?

The single question I asked myself in that moment that changed the trajectory of my entire life in the most ineffable ways, in ways I could never ever imagine even in my wildest dreams was, "WTF is wrong with you that you keep choosing these toxic men?"

I could have blamed them. That's easy. There was plenty of toxicity to go around between the two of them, but the most confronting thing, the raw truth of the matter, I chose them. Me. So the real question was, what was wrong with me that caused me to choose and marry people like that? I felt broken. A complete hot mess.

Here is the thing I want you to know , I was not broken and neither are you. But there was definitely something wrong within me and that is what I set out to explore, to understand, and then to do. Whatever… It… Took to change that.

I am one persistent willful woman. Let me tell you, I was obsessed with getting the answers and I did.

That old part of me who chose those kinds of men had to die for the real me to be reborn. The me who wrote this book, the me who had to become the role model she needed for herself because she did not exist. I had to unlearn all the lies I had taken on as truths about myself, about my value, about my worthiness, and about what I deserved.

Here are some of the questions I asked myself about myself that were not always easy because it can be very confronting to reveal to yourself all the ways you have gotten in your own way. All the ways you have lied to yourself, all the ways you have let yourself down to "keep the peace", all the ways you have chosen to please someone else, only to feel like you betrayed yourself in doing so, again and again, and again.

There is no way to sugarcoat it. It might be uncomfortable and confronting, but it is even more empowering. It is your key to your liberation and freedom from the bondage, boxes, and cages your past experiences have unknowingly made that you put yourself in.

Here are some questions I want you to ask yourself privately. This is the time to be real, raw, and honest, don't lie to yourself, this is for you.

- Who am I really? Not who does my father/mother/ex/friends/society tell me I am or who I should be, but who am I really, outside of my roles?

- Am I sincerely, authentically, unapologetically being the real, weird, quirky, unique person that I am all the time?

- Or do I hide parts of myself? For fear of judgment or being criticized or fitting in.

- Why? What am I afraid of?

- What is your inner dialogue? How do you talk to yourself? If it's negative, would you speak that way to someone you love? So why do you speak to yourself that way? (this one is an eye-opener) No amount of negative self-talk will ever give you a beautiful life.

- Do I say yes to appease others when I really want to say no? Or vice versa, in other words, are you a people pleaser?

- Do I seek to validate myself through others' perceptions of me?

- Do I put others' needs ahead of mine to my own detriment? There is being of service and there is being a doormat, they are not the same.

- Do I tend to give and give and give and accept no reciprocation or very little in return?

- Do I like myself? What do I like about me? If I don't, why not?

- What messages did I get about myself as a child?

- Who wasn't there for you at a young age?

- Was I told I was too much? Not good enough? Bad? Why couldn't I be more like "so and so"?

- Do I still believe that? If yes, why?

- Do I have boundaries with people? Do I stand up for myself or do I shut up to keep the peace, or am I too nice to avoid confrontation, or "be the better person"?

- Do I try to save people and lose myself in the process?

- Did anyone teach you that love means pain?

- Do I tell people what I want or need or am I afraid to? And then expect them to read minds?

- Do I even know what I want in a partner or in a relationship? If not, what do you want?

- Do I honor, accept, and value myself exactly as I am right now? Not that we all can't be better, better is a beautiful word, but not at the price of devaluing yourself as you are now.

- Or do I chase some level of success, money, goals, some sort of "benchmark" and then when I have "that" then… and only then I will be worthy… valuable… good enough… happy.

I want you to understand something: You have always been good, worthy, deserving, and valuable. Your life experiences and the people in it have just caused you to not believe it or to doubt it.

Part of this journey of life is shedding the lies of the old you and unlearning all the false perceptions you unconsciously took on to reveal the truth that is you, that has always been you, the you who is perfectly made in God's own image and likeness. The newer, better you. The real you.

The Wins You Can't Buy

In a world obsessed with success that is measured by dollars, here's some success not celebrated enough.

Choosing yourself and get out of that toxic relationship.

Being audacious enough to speak the truth and what needs to be said lovingly.

Regulating your nervous system.

Taking personal responsibility and accountability for where you are in your life and no longer blame others.

Forgiving yourself for your past and give yourself compassion that you did the best you could with what you knew then.

Stopping people pleasing.

Caring more about what you think of yourself rather than what "they" think of you.

Removing yourself from all things, people, places, and experiences that bring you down.

Stopping the inner critic and become your own greatest cheerleader.

Taking time to nap, meditate, relax, pray, or do nothing, and fill up your own cup.

Nourishing your mind, your body, and your soul.

Being the first person to break generational unhealthy patterns and ways of being in your family.

Being a mother who chooses to stay at home and raise her children because that's what she *wants* to do.

The single mom or dad who does the best they can.

Being the brave warriors who pave a new path and don't follow what's popular or trending, they follow their own path.

Giving yourself so much love, acceptance, understanding, kindness, and compassion for who you are and how far you have come.

Working on becoming the best version of you.

Getting help in any area of your life.

Being authentic in a world of fake.

Choosing to see the "good" instead of the "bad."

Opening yourself up to love again even when it scares you.

Doing the work to heal your trauma.

Being kind to others.

Sharing your gifts with the world.

Following your own path.

Being the black sheep.

Having the courage to be disliked.

Take The Damn Nap

The hustle and grind in our modern culture is toxic and can make you miserable and eventually sick. Sometimes a nap is exactly what you need.

Pushing through to make sure you get all the things done on your endless to-do list can sometimes cause resistance. Be persistent in pursuing your dreams and desires, but also know when to rest. Your mind, body, and soul must be nourished and replenished.

So take a nap, take a day off, take a damn vacation. Have some fun, play, and enjoy yourself. You're not here to hustle and grind until you're dead or until you reach your so-called retirement age. Then what was it all for anyway?

Remember what it was like when you were a little boy or little girl? Yeah, tap more into that. "Except ye be like little children"

You are not here to suffer, to push through, or to work yourself to death. Your body needs rest to recover. Your soul needs rest to replenish. It's okay to stop, to be tired, to rest, and to do nothing.

Actually, sometimes the best thing to do is to do nothing. To do nothing is actually to do something. Be still. You don't always have to take action.

Action for action's sake sometimes makes you even more frustrated because you are trying to theoretically force an outcome, rather than allow it and follow inspired action. Often when you are willing to sit in the space of nothing "no thing" the silence, quieting the mind, in meditation or in a meditative state, that's when you get the best ideas, the most inspired action to take, this is when God can talk to you.

Sometimes the very thing you need to do is to lean back and trust that everything is going to be okay and that everything always works out for you.

You Are Not Broken

There was never anything really wrong with you even though I know many times it may have felt as though there was. You are literally an aspect of God, the creator of everything there ever was and ever will be seen and unseen. The creator of worlds is within you.

What is actually "wrong" is the lies you have taken on as truths about who you are, what you can have, what you are worth, what is your value, how much money you can have, what kind of relationship you can have, where you settle, where you play small, where you stay comfortable and complacent, the boxes and roles society and your environment has told you that you are like "this" makes you good, this makes you bad,. This makes you right and this makes you wrong.

Stop allowing yourself to hold on to these lies, to these false perceptions. It is time to unlearn all of that to shine the bright light that you are. If you are going through some hard times right now, then I promise you it's not to make you suffer, you are not bad or wrong and you certainly do not deserve it.

Often the hard times, the "dark" times are trying to show you all the ways you have taken on other people's false perceptions of who you are and what you deserve, and the pain you feel is your soul assisting you in shedding those lies from your being so you can release them once and for all.

Let everything that wants to go, go, let everything that wants to come, come. Allow your divine nature to shine through.

From out of the darkness, you come into the light. You are innately good, you are valuable, you have always been worthy and deserving of a beautiful life. The power that creates worlds is within you.

Don't you think it's about time you started acting like it?

Sometimes the Wrong Partner is a Gift

Choosing the wrong partner can destroy you if you let it. But here's the gift if you are willing to see it and allow it.

They are a mirror within you of all the ways you have:

Devalued yourself

Denied yourself

Made yourself unworthy

Made yourself not good enough

Felt like you needed to earn love

Given your love to people who are takers and users

Tried to fill the void within you with them

Abandoned yourself

When we have unaddressed wounds, we will attract the same in another. Not in a form of punishment, to "show you" the wound so that you may heal it.

You see these were never true but sometimes our caregivers (mother and father) unconsciously project this onto us when we are young and impressionable and it literally becomes our "truth", our personality, encoded into our nervous system, this perception of self.

And then it runs how we think, how we feel, what we believe to be true about ourselves and others, and it becomes our auto-pilot, a program, a way of being that can often go unnoticed until a person, a relationship, an event brings it back up to be healed.

Once you can "see" this, once you are aware, you can start to shed all those untruths, evolve and heal your nervous system, shift your conditioning and consciousness, and finally feel and embody the love, and be the powerful being that you have always been.

That God has made you to be.

Pray From Your Power, Not from Your Pain

Most people don't know how to pray properly which is why their prayers are not answered, now I'm not saying I am an expert in prayer, but I know how I used to pray versus how I pray now has significantly changed and improved and I have come to have a deeper understanding and wisdom that I want to share with you.

Most pray from pain and suffering and a "please, please, please" make this thing or situation go away, by begging. Do you think Jesus prayed from that place? Did he beg? No, he prayed from his power. He knew when he asked, it was always given.

He knew, *I and my Father are One but my Father is greater than I.* He knew that through God anything and everything is possible. And so in that knowing or gnosis, he commanded (think certainty, think expectation) that what he wanted was already his and he gave thanks and rejoiced in it even when he couldn't "see" it.

Most people's prayers are pathetic and weak; that's the truth of it. Most people, and in the past, I did too, pray from lack and fear and that's why it doesn't work. The power that runs to and through you, the power that creates worlds is not weak, groveling, and pathetic. There is no lack in God. Look around you at all of God's creations. There is no such thing as a lack in God.

The truth is your potential to *be, do,* and *have* whatever you want has always been there and always will be. It's just waiting for you to recognize and accept it.

This is one of the biggest lies we have ever been told by people who want to benefit from your fear so you can be controlled and manipulated.

Microdose of Bitch

In nature, no wild mother brings her children up to be prey. She brings her children up to nourish themselves and avoid being prey. Only humans bring their children up to be prey and then create taboos and morality around nourishing themselves.

And we have so many inner taboos around us "You're a bad person", or "You're selfish"; be nice, be pleasing to those around you. "Don't be too much."

And this is why we grow up and we don't know how to nourish ourselves properly and nourishment for humans is wealth. It is ludicrous when you think about it to make people wrong or bad to have healthy ambition and healthy competition. It is who we are, it's in our blueprint, it's what evolution is all about.

But instead, we are conditioned to be good, giving, and pleasing. Nothing in nature is like this. Nature is full of ambition and competition, evolution in its purest raw form.

This turning into prey happens with both men and women, but especially women. As women, we are conditioned to be prey even more. But if you look at fashion, entertainment, and fame as examples, there is this microdose of bitch vibe personified.

These women are not prey, they are going to nourish themselves, and they thrive. Yet the normal everyday woman is not allowed to have this energy, if she dares try, she is labeled "wrong, bad, dirty, sinful."

Instead, we are encouraged to please, not be too much, to over-give, but don't receive, and make sure we are nice. These women are prey and in healing this "prey" conditioning, women usually go one of two ways: She either turns into a cold macro dose of bitch, or she plays the victim, becomes a manipulator, and/or seeks to be rescued.

The year 2020 began showing you the stakes of being prey, it was a wake-up call. It's time you found your microdose of bitch and nourished yourself.

It's time for you to embody power, to be bold, audacious, well-nourished, and thrive. Allow your diva and bad bitch to rise.

The Courage to Love

Most people don't even know how to love, so we love selfishly and with conditions or with barriers. That used to be me too.

The modern dating world of love and relationships is loaded with past pains of past lovers, people bleeding their old wounds all over each other, looking to fill this void of emptiness inside through going from partner to partner, relationship to relationship, porn, vapes, alcohol, work addiction, gambling, drugs, social media, and television. *Anything* to keep ourselves distracted from feeling the pain of loss, grief, sadness, and longing because it feels like it's too much. Sometimes it makes us feel like we're going to die. So instead of feeling those emotions, those sensations, we become slaves to the distractions that keep us from feeling *too* much. Basically, we chase fake hits of dopamine or we numb out.

Instead of opening our hearts to let love in, we shield ourselves from the potential of heartbreak because the rejection of not being loved fully for who we are is too much.

Often this stems from our past experiences with our caregivers, mothers or fathers who either did not or could not give us the love we deserved because they were unable to, meaning many of the times they didn't know how because they never learned from their own parents. Usually, this is an ancestral pattern of behavior that the family takes on unconsciously and keeps handing it down until someone changes it for good. It becomes so deep within our somatic experience, within our bodies we feel this fear of not being loved, rejected, or abandoned again in our adult relationships.

Yet one of the things we all long for and desire is love. We are love. It is our core essence. We were birthed from love from God, our Creator. The entire world we live in is a creation of love.

To love is the greatest risk of all. We risk rejection, betrayal, loss, and pain, yet if we have never loved truly, madly, deeply, have we ever even lived? I say no. If we have not allowed our hearts to be obliterated open to feel the depth of true love, the deepest, most intimate profound connection of experiencing the love of our lives, what are we even doing here?

Reflect here for a moment: How are you loving yourself? Do you even like yourself? Or do you constantly allow the mind chatter to tell you all the ways you are unlovable, not good enough, and undeserving? Doing this cuts you off from the love you seek.

So the next time an uncomfortable emotion arises within you, I want you to try this instead: Allow yourself to go into the body and feel all your sensations when they arise in whatever is there. Be present fully with the emotion, sensation, or negative feeling you are experiencing and then allow yourself to feel. Feel it all! Feel the anger, the betrayal, the rage, the grief, whatever your emotion is, and *let it out*.

You can let it out and express it through tears, laughter, screaming, breaking something, throwing some coconuts, or yelling it out, do whatever it takes, but please don't hold it in anymore. Let it out, express it, and stop holding it in and taking it out on yourself, it's poison and will destroy you if you let it. You can do any of these in the safety of your own house or go out in the middle of nowhere and do this, or in nature too.

Often when we are dating and relating, we don't realize that there is nothing more triggering and has the opportunity for healing than a romantic relationship if you let it. You can do all the "personal development" work you want alone and I highly encourage it because we all have our own inner work to do, but there is a place in union, in romantic love that will feel deeply uncomfortable, because nothing pulls out your core wounds that need healing like romantic love. Those parts that come up and you think wtf I thought I healed that shit?!

True love, the love of your life, can feel like a death at first because your heart is being ripped wide open, with nowhere to hide anymore because that's exactly what it is, the death of the old self and the merging into another into true love.

Let's be real, most of us have never experienced or seen a healthy love modeled in our lives. If that's you, please start by loving yourself, especially the parts the world has told you are bad or wrong, start with those, those are your core wounds and your biggest opportunity for transformation. Start changing the inner talk from critic to cheerleader, more praise, more acceptance, more compassion, more understanding, more forgiveness for you by you.

A couple questions to ponder: How can you allow yourself to be cracked wide open to love even more? How can you love more truly, madly, and deeply?

You're Enough, Now What?

What would you do today if you knew you were worthy of what you wanted right now?

What would you do today if you knew that you were deserving of what you wanted right now?

Of the love, of the relationship, of the life, of the happiness that you have always wanted right now?

With nothing to prove to anyone, nothing to do, exactly as you are now.

What would you do if you had absolute certainty that that was true?

Good enough right now

And that it was easy to get what you wanted

Exactly as you are

With fearless faith

What would you do?

How would you show up today in everything you do?

Who would you be?

What would you do differently?

Dumb Stuff We Tell Ourselves

Have you ever heard this one? "If it's too good to be true it probably is."

That's one of the most ignorant lies we have ever convinced ourselves is true. It often comes from a place of lack, not-enoughness, guardedness, and fear, self-protection from previous "bad" experiences. Although a guarded heart may prevent you from experiencing any more broken-heartedness, it will certainly also protect you from any true love.

To feel good is what you have always wanted and is the core of who you are. You have just been hanging around with people who have forgotten that, they have forgotten this about themselves. They have been hurt by other people who made them feel that this couldn't possibly be true.

Many of us have been told that we are "bad" since we were little children. "That's bad. You're bad. Why are you so bad? You're a bad boy. You're a bad girl."

You don't think this had an impact on you? The people you were biologically born to trust and love and to keep you safe, your caretakers, usually our mother and/or fathers telling you all the ways you were bad, or not good enough, etc.

If you didn't do as they said, well you were very aware that they had all the food and shelter, so you listened, you had no reason not to and if you were told these negative things enough, you began to believe them. Your subconscious mind absorbed them.

But I want to remind you of something: You are God's highest creation so that makes you innately "good", in fact, born already good, worthy, valuable, and deserving.

Start talking to yourself better, with more care, more kindness, your innate goodness that is you. Here are some I love:

I am blessed

Everything always works out for me.

I love you.

Look at everything you have done, look at who you have become.

You have such a big, beautiful heart.

You are safe, I've got you, I'll always have your back.

Try some out for yourself. Test them out. Feel them within your body, as if you are trying on a piece of beautiful clothing. Try it on, and see how it feels. If you don't like it, try some other words of praise. Find love and acceptance for every aspect of yourself.

And if that doesn't inspire you, maybe this beautiful scripture will.

Philippians 4:8 (NIV): *Finally, brothers and sisters, whatever is true, whatever is noble, whatever is right, whatever is pure, whatever is lovely, whatever is admirable — if anything is excellent or praiseworthy — think about such things.*

You Have to First Be "The One"

I often tell people that if they want to find the one, they have to become the one.

I think most people don't understand what I mean by that. So what do I mean by that? We often have this "list" of our "perfect person". A checklist if you will, sometimes it's mental, and sometimes we write it down.

It is usually based on what the modern trends are or on what is popular. Some examples I see often are:

For women, it can tend to have to do with the man's status and power. He has a lot of money, he has a certain kind of career or what is perceived as highly successful, drives a certain kind of car, has a certain kind of home, and can provide them with a certain lifestyle they desire like travel, gifts, entertainment, etc. No judgment, strictly my observation living in our modern times and talking and working with all the people I do.

Now you know I am generalizing right now and this isn't *all* women, however as I have a very unique perspective than most. I see and hear things that many do not.

Then you have the men. They want her to be hot, sexy, great body, slutty, they often love it when their male friends are envious of them. So this is part of the draw of a woman being arm candy, often she is younger than him, and sometimes significantly, men usually don't care how much money she makes, in fact, often men prefer that women don't make a lot of money, not more than him anyway.

Then the classic thing we see repeat over and over again: the guy gets taken for a ride for his money and the girl gets called a gold-digger. Yet they both knew exactly what they were doing, they were both in it for what they could get out of it. For her, it was the money and for him, it was the sex with a hot young chick. Then both sides complain about the other stating, "no good ones" are out there.

There are a few reasons why people struggle to find the right partner, and one big one is that most don't even know what they actually want. They're vague, too general, hoping for "someone amazing" without clear specifics. Clarity is key here.

Another factor? Many people want someone who's not even a real vibrational "match" for them.

So, let's start by getting honest: Who are *you*, and what do you really bring to this so-called "table" everyone talks about? And no, I'm not talking about sex — that's a given in any healthy relationship.

Here's the real issue. Most people either don't know what they want at all, or they set sky-high expectations that don't match who they really are, or what they really bring to the table. Even more often, they are weighed down by the leftover pain from past relationships, clinging to an ex's memory instead of letting themselves find the connection they truly crave.

To help you get clear, ask yourself these questions:

What qualities do you genuinely bring to the table?

How do you treat others and yourself?

What's your current relationship with yourself really like?

How do you see relationships, and what do you truly want in a partner?

Do you align with those qualities you're looking for or naturally complement them?

And, finally, what are your deal-killers?

These answers will start to give you the clarity — and the power — to attract what you're actually looking for.

Sometimes Your Intellect Is Overrated

The body always knows when something isn't right or when it is right, but we override it with our intellect, our mind, and reason.

When you wake up do you have to tell your heart how to beat? Do you have to tell your lungs how to breathe? Or do they just do their thing? When you are cut, do you have to tell your body how to heal that cut or does it just go to work right away and start healing it without any help from your thoughts?

I know those seem like silly questions, right? So why is it that we don't listen to how we feel within our body more often?

When we are stressed or anxious, we feel it. When we are angry or irritated we feel it. Sometimes we feel this in our belly or womb area, our gut, and sometimes we feel it in the space just between our rib cage (solar plexus).

We usually feel some kind of sensation, but what do we do instead of tuning into it? We ignore it, override it, stuff it down, and suppress it.

Our body's intelligence is infinitely wiser than our brains, but we have been trained, conditioned, and brainwashed even to ignore that inner wisdom, to not feel, to disconnect, and therefore become even more detached from ourselves, each other, and our humanity. When it hasn't been safe to "feel," when a feeling has felt like "too much" from our past experiences, we will then begin to live in our heads — think overthinking.

This has been especially true for men, but it does occur in women because I used to live like that. You become an overthinker because your mind is trying to protect you and figure out the ten different ways this situation can go wrong to protect you from repeating past painful experiences.

So what's the solution? Start by allowing yourself to feel any sensation that arises in the present moment, and listen to the wisdom and intelligence of your body, be with the sensation, in other words, allow yourself to feel the uncomfortableness of it as it arises (no one ever died from feeling, but they did by not feeling), love and accept this sensation or emotion, meaning don't fight it or make yourself bad or wrong for feeling it, have compassion and understanding for yourself.

I also want to remind you of something that will help alleviate some of the overthinking, God did design us, after all, including our bodies and it runs itself without any interference from our thinking mind telling it what to do or how to do it.

Can you imagine if we had to actually direct our bodies to do all the things it just does perfectly and seamlessly? As brilliant as we are, we couldn't even fathom how to do that.

Back to the solution. Feel *all of it*. All the feels inside of your body, especially the uncomfortable stuff. That's where the deepest transformation is. Interesting isn't it? It's in what feels like the scariest place.

I hate to use this cheesy line but I'm going to do it anyway because it's perfect for what I am saying…

You have to feel it to heal it… and once you can start to allow more of that, you are on your way to feeling good more often.

What Are You Really Expecting from Love?

You get exactly what you expect in relationships and normally that's not a good thing, because we usually anticipate and expect the worst. That may be hard to hear.

So many of us speak so much for our own limitations, lack, and blame. But you see, you must be willing to examine yourself within. You can only receive what you see yourself receiving.

What are your thoughts and beliefs about relationships?

What are your attitudes around men and women?

Examine your own beliefs.

Listen and pay attention to your own thoughts, not for criticism or judgment, get curious, and take notice. Write them down to really "see" them. Scientists say we have roughly 60,000 - 70,000 thoughts a day. There is always a pattern of thoughts… consistent thoughts, repeating thoughts. What are yours around love, dating, and relationships?

What is your pattern or belief about yourself? Is it more positive or negative? Usually, it's a mix of both, but if you are being "realistic" and completely honest with yourself for most people it is mostly negative. So start writing all these patterns of thoughts down, and answer the questions above.

And while you are doing this, I want to offer this reminder: you are not your thoughts, unless you consciously are placing thoughts into your consciousness. If your thoughts are loaded with negativity and telling you all the ways you suck or are not good enough, then it's not you, it's your mother, your father, your step-parent, the bully in school, or a previous teacher, your ex and none of it is true.

You have to examine your own thoughts, beliefs, and so-called "truths" because you didn't put them there.

You took them on from your environment unconsciously, some empowered you and some disempowered you. Look within and examine everything. For the sake of yourself, and your current or previous relationships, write down your thoughts and examine them and how they make you feel.

Does it feel good or bad, not uncomfortable, the growth and evolution of self is always within the uncomfortable, so that's not what I'm referring to when I ask if it feels "bad."

Now look at your past experiences that went "wrong". What were you expecting in that relationship? What was your dominant train of thought? Your belief about yourself and/or them?

Quick story to help you understand. I grew up feeling and believing I was unworthy of anything "good", unworthy of being fully loved for who I am, not good enough, therefore that is all I could create in my life... mirrors and manifestations of the same being reflected back to me.

I believed I was unworthy, that I had to prove my value and therefore that is exactly what life gave me, people who made me feel I needed to prove my worth, toxic unhealthy relationships until I understood what I am sharing with you here and now and not only understood but just as importantly I put it into practice. This requires doing things differently.

You must examine your inside world to change your outside world. Make no mistake, if you find yourself in relationships with the "wrong" people, some part of your being is attracting it. It's not because you are bad or wrong but by way of some unexamined subconscious, unconscious beliefs. It is often what we are used to from our past experiences.

It's not the relationship with the "other person" that is the problem, it is the relationship with your Self. There is and never was anything "wrong" with you. It is your thinking that is wrong, your beliefs, your expectations, and your perceptions.

Intellectual knowledge about this does not bring results, words don't teach. It's what you do with the words that teach, and begin to prove everything I share with you in this book. Prove it to yourself by trying them out. Show yourself just how powerful you are.

Deal With It

Here's the issue with dating right now… everyone wants to point the finger and blame or shame the other. It's guys who suck or women who suck. Here's the real deal, if you are experiencing anything you don't want in your dating life or your relationships, then it's time for some deep introspection. You have to be the One before you can ever attract or find the One. It's always an inner game. Complain all you want but it does nothing to solve the issue. Do the work within and the rest will take care of itself.

In my own experiences and throughout all my years of teaching love, dating, and relationships, the one thing I see again and again is the relationships we have with ourselves are the one that needs the care, the love, the attention, the acceptance, the respect, the appreciation, the praise, the compassion, the understanding, and the forgiveness the most. The rest will then take care of itself.

Know Thyself

People will like you and they won't like you, it will have absolutely nothing to do with you and everything to do with them. People can only perceive you at the depth they have perceived themselves. Their perspectives, perceptions, and judgments of you come from within themselves where they have been judged or judged themselves. Rather than be introspective and learn about themselves and become better, the easier, lazier thing to do is blame, shame, and judge another.

When you are the most authentic truest version of yourself, you can care less about what "they" think. Not because you're some kind of an asshole, although some may think that, but who cares. On the contrary, you are so good with yourself, you know exactly who you are, you are your most authentic unapologetic unique self, and you like yourself, actually no, you love yourself fully, and accept all parts of you. You then care more about what you think of yourself, than what "they" think of you. Because no matter how great you are, not everyone is going to like you and that's okay; you're not pizza. You're not for everyone.

The only question is: what do you think of you? That's all that matters. Otherwise, you just end up morphing into everyone else's idea of you and then you wake up one day after years have gone by and don't even know who TF you are anymore.

You Didn't Deserve It

It's not your fault. If anything bad ever happened to you as a little boy or a little girl it's not your fault. I grew up without my dad, and I had many stepdads. I remember feeling and believing as a young girl that there must be something really wrong with me that everyone keeps abandoning me.

I used to think it was my fault. I wish I would have known then what I share with you now.

If you ever felt unloved, unsafe, or unaccepted as a child

It's not your fault

If you ever felt lonely and afraid as a child

It's not your fault

If anyone ever hurt you

It's not your fault

You didn't do anything wrong

You didn't deserve that

Sometimes in our childhood, we experience hurtful things, bad things, terrible things, and sometimes traumatic things from our caregivers and then we blame ourselves for it unknowingly because we can't understand the complexity of why people do the things they do. We then believe, "There must be something wrong with me" or "I must have deserved this." We internalize it as true and we believe that we are innately bad, wrong, broken, and unlovable

If we carry these thoughts into our adult lives (which many of us do unknowingly) we will inevitably attract people into our experiences who make this seem true. We seek out what we know (no matter how messed up) because the known is comfortable. Then prove it to ourselves again and again, as evidence of, "See I knew I was bad, wrong, broken, and unlovable, etc."

It's not true and it's not your fault what happened to you. You were in survival mode. Forgive yourself for the things you did or did not do in survival mode. You didn't know. It's not your fault.

Please know that you are good, you are valuable, you are lovable, you belong, you are wonderful, you are amazing.

You are a work of art.

You are a masterpiece.

Be Her King, Not Her Pawn

Dear Men:

Do you know what she really wants? She wants you to be a man of integrity, meaning; mean what you say and say what you mean.

What is the Sexiest Thing a Man Can Ever Do?

Exactly what he says he's going to do.

Your words and actions align and when you notice that they don't, you have enough self-awareness and integrity that you can also call yourself out, apologize, and do better.

She wants to feel the openness of your heart, the depth, and the devotion to her and her only. She wants you to make love to her slowly some days and other days, she wants you to rip her clothes off and throw her up against the wall and ravish her. Some women might be appalled by this, usually the feminists, and women who are still operating under their conditioned false selves, but deep down she knows it's true because it's about love, not force.

She wants to feel the exaggeration of your masculinity merging with her femininity. She wants to fully let go, trust, and surrender in to you.

This isn't about what you say, although sometimes words are spoken, it's about who you *are*. She can feel that, whether it is genuine or not. That's part of her gift, sensing and seeing the unspoken and the unseen. She wants you to be the protector in the physical realm and know that she is your protector in the spiritual realm.

She wants to feel your strength and leadership and true authentic God-given masculinity but know that if you cannot and will not lead, she will, and when she leaves you or loses respect for you, you will have no one else to blame besides yourself.

She wants a peaceful warrior, and in that peace, she also knows you will kick someone's ass if you need to protect her.

She wants a man who knows himself and dares to be himself no matter what "they" think ("they" includes her and family and friends).

She wants to be a priority in your life, don't make her guess if she matters, you will lose her. You must also understand she wants you to be a priority in your own life.

She wants you to plan the date and tell her what time to be ready and what to wear... or better yet, buy her that sexy dress and shoes and have it waiting for her.

She wants you to have the balls to call her out in a respectful way... stop being so passive.

Your ability to lead won't be trusted if you cannot trust your own ability to lead, and when you are passive that's what you are saying without words.

She wants to know everything about you, your deepest, darkest secrets, she wants to know your soul, your heart real, raw, and vulnerable.

She wants to know your mind, your body, and your soul.

She wants a man who is a true partner... she wants divine union.

She wants to be loved in the deepest, most profound, and devotional way and give that back to you.

She wants the greatest love story ever told.

She will be your greatest ally and your greatest cheerleader, she will always believe in you even when you have forgotten how to believe in yourself.

It seems like this man is elusive in today's modern society, but he's out there, he's in you, men, he's in every man... dormant, but he's been dying inside. He desperately needs to be unleashed... to awaken. Our world needs this man more now than ever.

But don't do it for the world. Don't even do it for her. Do it for you.

This is the magnetic man, a King... a true high-value man. It's time to become him.

Rise or Run

When it comes to romantic relationships, most men are not actually running away from good women. What is actually happening on a higher spiritual level is he is unconsciously running away from who he would have to become to be in a relationship with this kind of woman.

A great woman, the kind of woman every man truly craves and desires at the depth of his heart and soul, the kind of woman most men have not experienced yet in this lifetime, yet his soul recognizes her will require way more out of him than he may be willing to see or be in himself *yet*.

She will call him forward into his true purpose, she will call him forward into his highest Godself and she doesn't do this with words, it is her presence, her essence that calls him forward.

This is the gift of the embodied awakened feminine, the truth of her gift when she is a walking embodiment of the woman God made her to be. But, for the man who is not ready to face himself and all the ways he is denying his own greatness, this kind of woman may cause him to run.

She sheds the light on his shadows, of where he has been playing small, where is leaking his energy, where he has no boundaries, where he is still playing nice, passive, and pleasing. For the man who is not ready to "see" that in himself, the man who is not ready to have the mirror held up to him, because that's what she is, his egoic mind that needs to control everything will cause him to run away.

She is there to shed light on his darkness, not evil, the negative beliefs he still holds about himself, she is a light worker, here to shed the light onto the darkness and he has two choices: rise or run.

This isn't just any woman; this is the woman who has become the phoenix rising from her own ashes. She has met her own darkness and transmuted it into her light. No one saved her, she has her own heroine codes, and she has turned her deepest pains into her deepest passion, purpose, and love. She knows, accepts, and loves herself fully. She is the truth and the light, she understands her own Divine nature and yours, all of Creation from the Creator, God, and she is in deep devotion to this path of love.

This is ancient energy, this is the energy that has been missing from the world, from women, it has been considered taboo and shamed intentionally to disempower.

If you look historically, the greatest men in history who have ever existed became their greatest and discovered their true genius when they had the love of a great woman, the right woman. This kind of woman.

There is a reason the saying exists "Behind every great man there is a great woman."

You don't have to believe me, research it yourself, and find the truth yourself.

So the only question left to ask for you men is: What are you going to do, rise or run?

And women I invite you to explore deeper within yourself how you can peel away the layers of protection and become even more of your core feminine essence.

Why Wing It?

Did you know that the most successful people, those who have achieved extraordinary lives, have all had coaches or worked with mentors along the way?

Why not you? Being a lone wolf is actually a trauma response. No one ever got to any true measure of success in life alone. No one.

Why should your relationships be any different?

Did you grow up with perfect parents who were examples of a perfect relationship and a perfect love?

Probably not and even if you did, how are your relationships going for you?

How did you learn how to have a successful, healthy relationship? Trial and error, or friends' advice from who is or was in the same boat, magazines like Cosmopolitan, or watching old shows like Sex in the City. According to divorce statistics, the success rates of having hot, happy, and healthy relationships, hell even one part of that trio, just plain suck.

If you are like most people, your relationships may have ended in divorce or a nasty breakup, leaving you resentful. That resentment convinces you that you are broken, or they are, and then you either settle into another mediocre relationship because it is better than being alone. You may give up on love altogether, but why choose that path instead of seeking help from an expert.

Did you know that the person you choose to be your partner will have the greatest impact on your life? You will spend more time with them over your lifetime than anyone, including your children and your colleagues, your family, and your friends. And that person will have the biggest impact on your quality of life. They influence how much wealth you create, how successful you become, your mental and physical well-being, and your overall happiness, or lack thereof.

The "wrong one" can cost you everything; your sanity, your peace of mind, your children, your mental health, and your bank account, and even worse for some.

The "right one" — well, those who have the "right one" know. They help you in creating together more peace, love, fulfillment, joy, wealth, success, fun, and if you want an empire.

The "right one" will be your greatest asset… your secret weapon. Yet you are still out there trying to figure it out alone, running around blindly. DIY'ing the most important choice you will ever make, swiping left and right, thinking it's a "numbers game" or whatever BS you continue to tell yourself only to feel more frustrated or hopeless. Reflect on your own life, you know it's true, and the proof is your track record or the results thus far of your romantic relationships.

Now, you don't need to keep winging it. You don't have to play this game blindfolded anymore. The best relationships aren't just thrown together by luck; they're built with intention, with clarity, and yes, with a little help from someone who's walked the path.

Cave, Cocoon, Comeback

I notice a lot of personal development teaching has one unhealthy thread to it. It's this perception that being alone, independent, lone wolf, this part that says basically you can do this alone. And of course, we can, meaning we are physically able, and at the same time, we are not solitary creatures.

We do not thrive alone or in isolation. We are tribal communal beings who thrive best when we are together. We thrive in union, in love, in intimacy, in connection, in giving and receiving love.

And sure, in the beginning of doing any inner work, personal development work there is a period of just wanting to be alone. But then you're going to want to be around your tribe, your people and this sometimes looks different than the tribe before.

Some people come along with you on this journey and others fall off and then new people come to join. So when you start doing this inner work, the healing, the unlearning, the unbecoming of all you are not, the removing of the limiting beliefs, the false perceptions, the judgments, who "they" said you were. "They" means your family, your friends, religion, government, culture, TikTok, Instagram, Facebook, the bully at school, the asshole boss, the ex, etc.

And you feel the need to go into hiding, into your cave, into being alone, know that it is part of the process. So honor it and don't forget to come out and keep your heart open and then get back out there.

Just like a caterpillar goes into a gooey mess inside the cocoon and then comes out of it a beautiful magnificent butterfly, so must you to go through a transformation. It is your initiation into your best self.

Your highest self… your most authentic expression.

Cut the Crap, Feel the Truth

If you're in your head and overthink a lot it's probably because at some point, or multiple points, it became too much for your nervous system. This is why so many of us are disembodied and disconnected. But we are built to feel, it is part of the wonderfulness of being a human and being in this body temple. In feeling the sensations, there is a point where we need help integrating the feeling of too much within our nervous systems and that's where an expert coach or therapist can help. You have to feel safe in your body first. You can start small right now on your own with what I am about to share with you next.

So in each moment of your life on a daily basis allow yourself to start to feel more, to feel all of it, the love and the sadness, feel the uncomfortable sensations, and try your best to just be present, with nothing to do, just breathe into wherever it is located within your body. Our lives are beautiful gifts and it's meant to be felt in its entirety. When we feel "bad" it can often be indicative of the stories we tell ourselves about what this feeling bad means, feelings of guilt or shame or embarrassment for example.

So start trying to feel whatever sensation arises in each moment that it presents itself without the usual story, attached to it. For example, when you feel triggered, is an excellent time to do this exercise. Feel into it with a childlike curiosity, like hmmm what's this all about? Why am I feeling this way? What story or thought am I believing? What's this all about? Heighten your awareness. Pay attention to the thoughts and beliefs that surface during these opportunities and then start to examine them. The majority of the thoughts you think aren't true and aren't even you… it's something your mother said, your father said, that bully said, that mean teacher said, your sibling said, your ex said… it's not you.

Then also ask yourself is this belief, this thought, this trigger serving my greater good? In other words, the kind of life you are desiring to create during your lifetime, does it serve that achievement of that. Usually not. Start tuning out those that do not serve your greater good and tune into ones that do. Feed and replace your thoughts and your mind with what you want, rather than with what is, or what was, or what you don't want any longer. The sooner you start tuning all of that noise out, the better off you will be. And the easier you will be able to tune into God's direction, your inner knowing, your north star.

First, you discover your "light"

Then you discover your "darkness"

And then you discover your true self

The Love That Strips You Bare

Dear Men:

How do you know? Love, that is. How do you know when it is right... when it is with the right person? When it is special... sacred

I'll tell you from a feminine perspective. It transcends anything your mind can fathom. It is this inner knowing that gnaws at your soul. Your mind cannot explain it, your body knows, your heart knows, your soul knows, you feel it, it is undeniable.

Often will scare you by just how naked and raw it makes you feel. Fully exposed, like someone has ripped open your heart for the whole world to see and there you are unprotected, exposed, and bare naked.

Yet you know you never have to protect yourself from this person, have never felt more alive, never felt closer to God, the feelings transcend all language... it is truly ineffable. It is a mind, body, heart, and soul connection, deep and sacred, the way of Love, the way God intended us to be together as One.

There is no casual sex in this realm, there is only love-making at its purest rawest, most beautiful form, void of you or me, and only a merging of *us*. It is beyond anything most of us have ever experienced but the thing we all deeply yearn for, crave, long for, want, and desire.

AND you are deathly afraid of it because most of us have never had a love like this, so vulnerable, intimate, and real. Yet it is unconditional love in its purest form.

It requires us to be fully seen in our entirety, our perceived flaws and failures, it strips away all the lies and exposes only the naked truth that you see only this man the way God sees him, perfect in his image and likeness.

She sees you in your humanity and your divinity. Who you have had to become because of your pain, the warrior, the good man that you are, the little boy who never got the love and acceptance he needed. The man who cherished the women in his life only to be hurt, used, or betrayed.

She sees *all* of you and says, *I love you; you are safe with me.* She will not judge, condemn, criticize, or control you. She would never hurt you. Her love is devotional and unconditional. She will hold your heart gently in her hands.

This love penetrates every ounce of your heart, mind, body, and soul. It is a sacred gift to be cherished.

This love will cause you to rise or run. Many of us don't know a love like this, we become selfish, jealous, and tyrannical, attracting the very thing we fear, and then inevitably losing the person.

We are taking our initiation in love during this life. When a woman loves you this way, she becomes devotional and loves you at a depth you have never felt. And if you have never felt a love so deep and so pure it may scare you because it will cause you to rise and become the man worthy of this devotion, the man God created you to be. (P.S. You have always been this man; the world has just made you forget.)

You may be her protector in the physical realm, but she is your protector in the spiritual realm.

This love is the Truth of who we are and what God put us here to be, to feel, and to experience, true divine sacred union, side by side as One.

Your thoughts = your beliefs = your perceptions = your reality

Heal. Not because you are broken. When the love arrives that you asked God for, you will be able to recognize it and not run away from it. Don't open their heart unless you plan on cherishing it like the sacred gift it is.

Quit Whining and Own Your Magic

Okay, before you read this, I want you to imagine these words are being delivered to you from your favorite auntie, your BFF, your favorite big sister, your fairy godmother, or whoever is your favorite person in the world.

Said yet another way... the person who loves you and is not afraid to hurt your feelings, the one who tells you what you need to hear, not what you want to hear.

The one who gives you love while simultaneously kicking you in your ass when you need it.

Ok got the picture in your imagination? Proceed to read some perhaps much-needed tough love for ya.

Stop Being Such a Victim!

If you don't like your life *do* something about it to change it.

Stfu with all the blame and pointing fingers at others, and look in the mirror. All change starts with you.

In hating and condemning someone else, you are hating and condemning yourself, and probably without you even realizing that.

You, me, we are the daughters and sons of the Most High, of God.

There is no victimhood in God. Look around you, look at nature, is there victimhood there? No.

The power, God, that creates worlds is within you and always has been. Don't you think it's about time to start acting like it?

Your victimhood is a trap, a lie, that keeps you stuck and disempowered and living in fear.

There is no fear in God… fear is "man-made" and is a lie.

The power that creates worlds… God… is forever within you, always has been, you have never been "alone".

It's the lie of separation that keeps you in fear rather than faith, trust, knowing, certainty… your power.

What are you afraid of anyway?

I'd actually be more afraid of getting to your deathbed riddled with remorse that you never really lived… you just existed… that you never really loved deeply… that you played it safe instead… you lived a life of mediocrity, of doing ok, of paying the bills, of getting by.

You know it's true. Your egoic mind is trying to keep you small, safe, comfortable, and complacent, the part that says "yea but, yea but" and speaks to your limitations because it wants to control outcomes, there is safety; it is the "known".

But your soul, your spirit, your higher self, your God-self is calling you out and calling you forward and my hope is that reading this is igniting something within you.

Be bold, be audacious, stand out with your weirdness, your uniqueness… love truly madly deeply in full surrender to the "unknown".

Because, love, on the other side of the "unknown" is everything you have ever wanted.

What do you have to lose? Oh yeah… an epic life!

When you bend over backward to please others — whether to fit in, keep the peace, feel loved, or feel accepted — you end up pleasing no one, especially not yourself. Instead of feeling better, it leaves you feeling even worse. Why? Because each time you put their happiness above your own, you're unconsciously telling yourself they matter more than you do. That they're more important. That's self-abandonment at its finest, and we both know that's not what you truly want. So, choose yourself first. The right ones will stay.

No is a complete sentence.

Having boundaries is an act of self-love and if anyone gives you pushback, they are manipulating you.

You can only attract to you and hold a love to the depth and quality that you love and accept yourself.

Heal so that when you do attract the kind of person you have asked God for, you will be able to see them through your true lens and not the filter of your past pains and disappointments.

Knowing your worth is far deeper than reading it on a page or in a book, or saying it to yourself. It is having the courage to dig deep into your psyche and see all the ways you haven't valued yourself and why and to pull those out by the roots for good.

Absolutely Unapologetic

One of the biggest problems or challenges I see in the dating and relationship world is… *you care too much.*

You care too much about what your mom thinks.

You care too much about what your dad thinks.

You care too much about what your kids think.

You care too much about what your friends think.

You care too much about what society thinks.

You care too much about what "they" think.

You care too much about what your social media friends and followers think

about your lover, your partner, your dating life, your romantic relationships,

and not enough about what you think of those things.

No one is you, so they can't possibly know what's best for you. Even in their best intentions and love for you, or in their given advice, it's your thoughts about yourself that matter most.

Let me ask you something: Are they (any of the people above) the ones sleeping with your lover? Are they the ones cuddled up next to them? Are they the ones you are waking up to and going to sleep next to? Are they the ones making love to them?

Are they the ones who live inside of your body and have the desires you have? Are they the ones who long for the kind of person your heart longs for? Are they the ones who can feel how you feel and have had the same experiences you have had and know the things you know and want that have shaped the kind of partner your heart and soul yearn for?

Even in their best intentions for you, the answer is always, no.

Because there is only one you, and only you can decide what or who is best for you and that starts with you trusting yourself and your own choices no matter what. So, stop living for "them" or their approval. Stop concerning yourself with do they like them or will they like them or their judgment of your choice of romantic partners.

It is not their life to live… they have their own life to live… so what they think does not matter.

All that matters is that they are good for you and to you and that you are into them and want to be with them.

Stop caring so much about what others think of you and your love life and start caring more about what you think of yourself and your love life.

Besides, others' perceptions of what they perceive to be best for you even in their best of intentions, even if they love you, can still only come from their experiences, thoughts, and beliefs based on the life they have lived, no one can truly know what or who is best for you besides yourself. That's why the most important thing you can ever do for yourself to have the best life possible is "know thyself."

People may not always like or agree with what you do, but here's the truth. It often has nothing to do with you. When you start caring more about what *you* think of yourself and begin to live in that place, happiness will follow. It's not about dismissing others; it's about knowing that if you don't like *you*, happiness can only be temporary. Prioritize your own opinion, and watch everything change.

Captain Save a Ho

Dear Men:

There's a new kind of woman awakening, a new kind of feminine rising and I promise you she's the one that you've been waiting for. She's the kind of woman you have not known in this lifetime. And I also promise you that you will have to be a different man, a new man, to attract her, to get her.

Your old ways will not work on this woman because she does not need to be rescued, *she does not need to be saved.*

And she's also not a man-hater, she's not a feminist, nor is she a damsel in distress. She is the Divine Feminine.

She is the woman God made women to be and if you cannot meet her where she is:

She will not go down to your level, she will simply walk away.

She has the kind of energy that calls you out and calls you forward.

She only sees you in your power, in your Divinity, as the king you are,

and that's who she speaks to when she sees you, whether you see it in yourself or not.

What this will cause within you depends on you. If you still have shadows or parts of yourself that are still carrying guilt, shame, unforgiveness, fear, or whatever else around you, in who you are around women, around your world, then this woman might shake you to your core.

She will feel like she is too much for you because in her presence you see those parts of yourself. You see your own darkness and darkness is not evil, that's not what I'm referring to here. It's all the parts that you've hidden from yourself that you've tried to hide from the world. But if you can be the man who is courageous enough to see the mirror that she holds up to you. She will be your greatest love. She will be a love that will feel otherworldly because it is a love that has been missing from our world, but it is the true, pure love that God created us to feel.

So, I invite you, men, to step into this space and become who you've come into this world to be and no longer let society tell you who you should be. Become the man God needs you to be.

Only when this happens, will you be able to be with your true queen. This is the kind of woman who is only available for a man who is a king.

Imagine this kind of woman in your life, in your bed, by your side. You have wanted this and she's called you here. There's no accident, no random moment in this.

You're reading these words because you've created this, woven it from your own deepest desires, calling you forward. So here you are, standing at the edge of everything you've asked for. Are you ready to step in and become the man she can't resist?

When Men Lose Their Balls and Women Grow Them

There's a war among the sexes that has been waged against you and you probably don't even know it. Our society is turning men into women and women into men and I am not even talking about the whole gender thing; making more men passive and feminine and making more women more masculine. And it is happening right in front of your face and you are falling for it.

It is making you hate each other. You have been convinced that you don't need a man because you can make your own damn money.

And men have been convinced that you don't need a woman because you can swipe on any dating app and have casual sex with anyone anytime or watch a porno or do anything else that drains your life force energy.

Men and women are being divided and conquered right out in the open but disguised as empowerment, disguised as success, disguised as better than, worthy of more, the grass is greener, better off alone.

It has become men and women hating each other, it has men and women being at odds instead of in harmony and collaboration.

Don't believe me? Look around. This is what it looks like right now in our modern world.

Women being more like men = Boss babe, hyper independent, I don't need a man, and controls and criticizes men, guarded and jaded, often a man-hater. Ladies, no "real man" wants this, you can't attract a real masculine man when you're the "man" acting out from a place of unhealed wounds.

Men being more like women = Passive, nice guy, no boundaries, who doesn't stand up for himself, pleaser, over giver, has left his balls in his woman's pocket.

Men- no good feminine woman wants this, it's a turnoff and makes her feel unsafe and untrusting in your ability to protect her and she will have zero respect for you and definitely won't want to have sex with you.

Men and women are pawns in the name of divide and conquer. Think about it… A masculine man is completely turned off by the boss babe because she's the man in the relationship therefore repelling him. A feminine woman is completely turned off by the nice passive guy because this makes her feel unsafe and untrusting in his ability to protect her.

So, where does this leave us?

Caught in a distorted version of empowerment that, at its core, is just another tactic to keep us from thriving in the connections we deeply crave. Society has been whispering lies in our ears, convincing us that we're better off alone, that strength means closing off, and that love means domination or submission instead of true partnership.

Men, your strength doesn't come from becoming passive, from letting your voice and vision fade into the background. A woman needs your strength, your presence, your ability to stand firm and true, not just for her, but for yourself. When you reclaim that, you're stepping back into your power as the protector and provider you were meant to be.

Women, your worth isn't in proving you don't need anyone or taking the reins in every aspect of life. True power is knowing how to let go when it matters, to allow space for your natural feminine energy to create, to receive, and to nurture without fear. A strong, grounded man doesn't compete with you — he complements you.

This isn't about going backward or assigning rigid roles. It's about embracing what makes us different to create a relationship that's more powerful than the sum of its parts. Stop letting society steal your joy by convincing you to abandon the very traits that make you irresistible to each other.

If we can wake up to this, there's still hope to heal the divide. There's still time to find our way back to each other — to a connection that's real, natural, and fiercely alive.

About the Author

Melanie Verstraete holds a Bachelor of Science degree and is certified as a Life, Sex, Love, and Relationship coach. Verstraete is also the founder of *The Wild Heart Life*, a no-BS coaching movement that guides men and women out of toxic cycles and into the love and success they've been craving.

Raised amidst dysfunctional relationship dynamics, she transformed her own rollercoaster experiences into a thriving practice that fuses raw emotional healing with real-world results. Known for her direct, witty style (with a big-hearted dose of compassion), Melanie helps clients ditch the old, outdated stories that keep them stuck, so they can embrace a life that's equal parts wild, loving, and unapologetically free.

Now, with her first book, *Pearls of Wisdom*, she's showing readers everywhere that "settling" is never the solution and that true transformation is closer than they think. Melanie's groundbreaking insights into love, dating, and relationships have landed her features on local and national TV, in prestigious magazines, and on numerous podcasts solidifying her as an influential expert.

www.ingramcontent.com/pod-product-compliance
Lightning Source LLC
Chambersburg PA
CBHW061602120626
46550CB00004B/1579